Black Americans in Autobiography

Black Americans in Autobiography

An Annotated Bibliography of Autobiographies and
Autobiographical Books Written Since the Civil War

Russell C. Brignano
Carnegie-Mellon University

Duke University Press   Durham, North Carolina   1974

Printed in the United States of America

Contents

Preface

This bibliography lists and annotates autobiographies and autobiographical books written by black Americans from the end of the Civil War to early 1973. In the annotations I have tried not to make value judgments on such matters as aesthetics, writing skills, and personal philosophies and beliefs. My purpose is to provide basic information about the authors' public lives and to identify some of the geographical locations where those lives were led. I make no claims that the annotations will satisfy everyone and that the bibliography has not overlooked titles. I do, in fact, invite suggestions and criticisms so that if in the future the bibliography is revised, and expanded to cover books published after early 1973, librarians, scholars, and students will have a better research tool.

The items in Section I, "Autobiographies," are volumes describing appreciable spans of the authors' lives. In Section II, "Autobiographical Books," are diaries, travelogs, collections of letters, collections of essays, eyewitness reports of public events, and narrations of relatively brief periods of time, all of which address some phases of the authors' lives. A few titles in this section do offer short autobiographical vignettes, but none has as its major purpose the telling of a life story. The third section, unannotated, is a checklist of autobiographies and autobiographical books written before the end of the Civil War and reprinted, or published for the first time, since 1945. Each section is arranged alphabetically by author, and consecutive numbering of items is continued from one section to the next. Where a single author has published more than one volume in a specific category, the entries are recorded by publication date, from the earliest to the latest.

Each entry item contains the following information: the author and, if applicable, the coauthor; whenever known, the author's year of birth and, if applicable and known, the author's year of death; the title (and subtitle); the volume number, if applicable; information about forewords, introductions, illustrations, afterwords, notes, bibliographies, and indexes; the place of publication; the publisher; the year of publication; the final-page number; reprint information, if applicable; symbols for up to ten known library locations (the list of symbols and corresponding libraries appears after Section III); the annotation; if applicable, a cross reference to other autobiographical volumes by the author or by a member of his family.

Following the list of library symbols are three indexes. They are keyed to the entry-item numbers in Sections I and II and to the annotations. The first index is for experiences, occupations, and professions. The second lists the geographical locations and educational institutions mentioned in the annotations. The last is the index of titles for all three sections.

Many published sources aided me in the compilation of this bibliography. Among the most valuable bibliographies were these: Louis Kaplan, *A Bibliography of American Autobiographies* (Madison, Wis.: Univ. of Wisconsin Press, 1962), listing and briefly annotating many autobiographies through 1945; Monroe N. Work, *A Bibliography of the Negro in Africa and America* (New York: H. W. Wilson, 1928); and Elizabeth W. Miller and Mary L. Fisher, *The Negro in America: A Bibliography*, 2d ed. (Cambridge, Mass.: Harvard Univ. Press, 1970). Extremely useful were the bibliographies dealing with black-American holdings of the libraries at the Florida Agricultural and Mechanical University, Florida State University, Hampton Institute, Lincoln University (Pennsylvania), Livingstone College, San Diego State College, and the University of Toledo. Also helpful were the published catalogs of the Schomburg Collection of Negro Literature and History at the Harlem Branch of the New York Public Library, 9 vols. (Boston: G. K. Hall, 1962; 2-vol. Supplement, 1967), the Arthur B. Spingarn Collection of Negro Authors at Howard University, 2 vols. (Boston: G. K. Hall, 1970), and the Jesse E. Moorland Collection of Negro Life and History at Howard University, 9 vols. (Boston: G. K. Hall, 1970). Indispensable was *The National Union Catalog*, as was the ambitious project *The National Union Catalog, Pre-1956 Imprints* (London: Mansell, 1968-1973). In its alphabetical arrangement by authors, the 274th volume, published in 1973, has reached only the letter J.

I could not have completed this bibliography without the diligent, thoughtful, and kind assistance of others. I owe them much. I began my research under the sponsorship of the National Endowment for the Humanities, which awarded me a Younger Humanist Fellowship for the academic year 1970-1971 to explore "The Aesthetics of Black-American Autobiography," a study I temporarily abandoned when I discovered that a dependable bibliography of primary sources had first to be assembled before my original project could be pursued. Without the help of the Endowment I would still be gathering materials rather than publishing this volume. Aiding me in different ways were many people, too numerous for all to be named here. Among them were librarians in the United States and Canada, publishing house personnel, and some of the authors themselves. I wrote over two hundred letters of inquiry, and the cooperation I usually received was gratifying. I visited the Hartford Public Library in Connecticut, and the libraries of Trinity College, the University of Wisconsin, the Historical Society of Wisconsin, and West Virginia University, and at each I was treated ably and generously. With much appreciation I remember James P. Johnson, a staff member at the Founders Library of Howard University, who served me cordially and efficiently when I journeyed to Washington in March 1972.

My most faithful and helpful assistants were in Pittsburgh. They are the librarians at the Hillman Library of the University of Pittsburgh, the Carnegie Library of Pittsburgh, and, particularly, the following staff members at the

Hunt Library of Carnegie-Mellon University: Ruth Corrigan, Margaret Kelley Deitzer, Dorothy Kabakeris, Dorothy Nicholas, Harriet Van der Voort, and Frieda White. I could ask for no more than what they expertly and cheerfully accomplished. An undergraduate English major at Carnegie-Mellon University, Ann Cornyn, painstakingly investigated for me some of the published sources cited above. And my friend and colleague Professor Eugene Levy of the History Department at Carnegie-Mellon suggested titles I had failed to uncover and then took valuable time from his own research at Fisk University to examine and annotate a rare volume I could not obtain.

My greatest indebtedness is to my wife, the former Mary Louise Germann. She not only provided astute and professional editorial assistance, but also lovingly offered what I was much in need of, patience, understanding, encouragement. She too seems to have endured.

R. C. B.

Carnegie-Mellon University
Pittsburgh, Pennsylvania

Black Americans in Autobiography

I. Autobiographies

1. Aaron, Henry "Hank" Louis (1934-   ). *"Aaron, r.f."* As told to Furman Bisher. Foreword by Furman Bisher. Illustrated. Appendix. Cleveland: World Publishing Co., 1968. 212p.

   *CtH   DLC   PPi   RP   Wa

   A professional baseball player, famous for his ability to hit home runs, focuses on his career, particularly with the Milwaukee Braves and the Atlanta Braves. He also occasionally refers to his youth in Mobile, Alabama, where he was born.

2. Abubadika, Mwlina Imiri [formerly Carson, Robert "Sonny"] (1935-   ). *The Education of Sonny Carson*. New York: Norton, 1972. 203p.

   CtH   DLC   PPi   PPiCl   PPiU   WHi   WU   WvU

   The head of the Brooklyn branch of the Congress of Racial Equality devotes much of his autobiography to describing his efforts in the 1960s for fostering community control over local educational and law-enforcement institutions. He also recalls his earlier life as a Brooklyn street-gang leader, a petty criminal, and a prison inmate.

3. Adams, Elizabeth Laura (1909-   ). *Dark Symphony*. New York: Sheed & Ward, 1942. 194p.

   CoDR   CtH   DHU   DLC   NN   NcD   ViHal   WU   WaSpG

   Permeating the author's account of her childhood and adolescence in California, mostly in Santa Barbara, is her quest for a religious faith, leading to her conversion to Roman Catholicism. She reveals as well her desire to attain success as a dramatist and poet.

4. Adams, John Quincy (b. 1845). *Narrative of the Life of John Quincy Adams, When in Slavery, and Now as a Freeman*. Harrisburg, Pa.: Sieg, Printer & Stationer, 1872. 64p.

   DHU   DLC   MH

   Adams' very brief narrative encompasses his slave life in Virginia, his escape to Pennsylvania during the Civil War, and his employment as a domestic and hotel worker in the Harrisburg area.

5. Aleckson, Sam (b. 1852). *Before the War, and After the Union: An Autobiography*. Boston: Gold Mind Publishing Co., 1929. 171p.

   DHU   DLC   MH   NN

   An ex-slave from South Carolina who served a Confederate officer during the Civil War, Aleckson tells of the significant events in his life through 1914. In 1876 he moved to "Spring Lake, New England" (probably Windsor, Vermont), where he was employed as a laborer.

   *For these symbols and the corresponding libraries, see the list that follows Section III and precedes the Indexes.

6. Anderson, Marian (1902-   ). *My Lord, What a Morning: An Auto-biography*. Illustrated. New York: Viking Press, 1956. 312p.

    Reprinted New York: Avon Publications, 1956.

    CSdS CtHT DHU FTaFA NN PLuL PPiCl PPiU WU WvU

    The famous concert singer and opera performer recalls her early life in Philadelphia, then describes the major events in her career.

7. Anderson, Robert (b. 1819). *The Life of Rev. Robert Anderson. Born the 22d Day of February, in the Year of Our Lord 1819, and Joined the Methodist Episcopal Church in 1839. This Book Shall Be Called the Young Man's Guide, or, the Brother in White*. Macon, Ga.: J. W. Burke, 1891. 116p.

    Revised and reprinted Atlanta: Foote & Davis, Co., 1900.

    CU DHU GM GU NN NcD TNF

    A Methodist Episcopal minister depicts his slave life in Georgia and his later religious work as a pastor and circuit preacher. He was also a whitewasher in Macon for twenty-five years. The 1900 edition of his autobiography features a preface detailing his ministerial duties after 1891 and his travel experiences in Florida and the Midwest. [See Item 294.]

8. Anderson, Robert (1843-1930). *From Slavery to Affluence: Memoirs of Robert Anderson, Ex-Slave*. Illustrated. Hemingford, Nebr.: Hemingford Ledger, 1927. 59p.

    DLC NN

    Born and reared a slave in Kentucky, Anderson served in the Union Army during the Civil War. Later he fought in the Indian Wars in Missouri, Kansas, Texas, and New Mexico. After working at various jobs in Iowa and Kansas, he settled in Nebraska, where he became a construction worker and farmer. His autobiography ends before 1890.

9. Angelou, Maya [formerly Johnson, Marguerite] (1928-   ). *I Know Why the Caged Bird Sings*. New York: Random House, 1969. 281p.

    Reprinted New York: Bantam Books, 1971.

    CtY GU IU KU MB OU OkU PPiU WHi WvU

    Later to become a fiction writer, dancer, actress, and journalist, Angelou here describes her childhood in a small Arkansas town and in St. Louis, moving then to her high school years in San Francisco. Her autobiography ends in 1945.

10. Armstrong, Henry [formerly Jackson, Henry] (1912-   ). *Gloves, Glory, and God: An Autobiography*. Illustrated. Westwood, N.J.: Fleming H. Revell, 1956. 256p.

    DHU DLC NN NcD OCl OkU PP TxU

    A boxer who simultaneously held world titles in three weight classifications speaks through the third person to describe his early life in Mississippi and St. Louis, the highlights of his boxing career, his successful bout with alcoholism, his religious conversion, and his missionary work as a Baptist minister in California.

11. Armstrong, Louis (1900-1971). *Swing That Music*. Introduction by Rudy Vallee. Illustrated. Music Section edited by Horace Gerlach. Glossary. New York: Longmans, Green, 1936. 136p.

     AzU CoU DHU FTaSU MB MiU NN OU PPi TU

     The popular jazz musician and singer recounts his rise to fame, beginning with his youth in New Orleans and closing at his musical successes in Chicago and New York City. [See next item and Item 297.]

12. Armstrong, Louis (1900-1971). *Satchmo: My Life in New Orleans*. Illustrated. New York: Prentice-Hall, 1954. 240p.

     Reprinted New York: Signet Books—New American Library, 1955.

     AzU CoU DHU FTaFA FU MB NN OU PLuL PU

     This lively account of Armstrong's first twenty-two years in New Orleans culminates with his playing in a major jazz band in Chicago. [See preceding item and Item 297.]

13. Arter, Jared Maurice (b. 1850). *Echoes from a Pioneer Life*. Illustrated. Atlanta: A. B. Caldwell Publishing Co., 1922. 126p.

     Reprinted Freeport, N.Y.: Books for Libraries Press, 1971.

     DHU GEU NcD NcU NjP TNF TxU ViHaI ViW WHi

     An educator, academic administrator, and Baptist minister, Arter begins his third-person autobiography by describing his slave life near Harpers Ferry, West Virginia. After the Civil War, he worked at various jobs, in West Virginia, New York State, Pittsburgh, and Washington, D.C. He studied at Storer College, Pennsylvania State College, Hillsdale College, and the Chicago Theological Seminary. He taught at Storer College, Baptist Theological Seminary (Lynchburg, Virginia), and Morgan College; was Principal of the Cairo (Illinois) Bible School and the Hill Top (West Virginia) Graded School; and later was President of the West Virginia Industrial School, Theological Seminary and College. His narrative includes a selection of his sermons.

14. Ashe, Arthur, Jr. (1943-   ). *Advantage Ashe*. As told to Clifford George Gewecke, Jr. Illustrated. New York: Coward-McCann, 1967. 192p.

     DHU DLC NN PPi

     The former Davis Cup tennis star focuses on his athletic career, opening at his teenaged years in Richmond and Lynchburg, Virginia, and in St. Louis, progressing through his college years at the University of California at Los Angeles, and his stint as an officer in the U.S. Army.

15. Atkins, James A. (1890-1969). *The Age of Jim Crow*. Index. New York: Vantage Press, 1964. 300p.

     DHU DLC NN PPiU WHi

Much of Atkins' life was spent as a U.S. Civil Service administrator and as a teacher. He recalls his early life in Knoxville, Tennessee, where he became a printer and a teacher. He was educated at Knoxville College, the University of Denver, and the University of Chicago; and he taught in the Denver public schools and at the Tennessee Agricultural and Industrial College. During the 1930s and World War II he served in the U.S. Office of Education and later worked for the U.S. Air Force near Denver. He also was active in the Denver Urban League and contributed articles to Denver newspapers. His autobiography includes many comments on racial attitudes and problems.

16. Bailey, Pearl (1918-   ). *The Raw Pearl*. Illustrated. New York: Harcourt, Brace & World, 1968. 206p.

Reprinted New York: Pocket Books, 1969.

CtH   DHU   DLC   PPi   PPiU   WU

The popular singer and actress portrays her early life in Virginia, Philadelphia, and Washington, D.C., before relating the significant events of her career in show business. [See Item 298.]

17. Banks, [Ernest] Ernie (1931-   ), and Jim Enright. *"Mr. Cub."* Foreword by Warren C. Giles. Introductions by Jack Brickhouse and Jim Enright. Illustrated. Appendix. Chicago: Follett Publishing Co., 1971. 237p.

CtH   DLC   PPi   RP

A professional baseball player, Banks recalls his youth in Dallas, his performances with Negro baseball teams, his U.S. Army service, and his major-league career, beginning in 1953, with the Chicago Cubs.

18. Barlow, Leila Mae. *Across the Years: Memoirs*. Montgomery, Ala.: Paragon Press, 1959. 84p.

DHU   NcD

A retired professor records her career at Alabama State College, where she had been chairman of the English Department from 1931 to 1957. She also touches briefly on her early life in Georgia, her education at Spelman College, and her years as a school teacher in Americus, Georgia.

19. Barnett, Ida B. Wells—see Wells, Ida B.

20. Barrow, Joseph Louis—see Louis, Joe.

21. Battle, Augustus Allen (1864-1928). *A Synopsis of the Autobiography of Rev. Augustus A. Battle*. Preface by J. B. Clayton. Washington: The Author, 1927. 15p.

DLC

In this short pamphlet the author sketches his early life in Alabama, his education at Talladega College, his ordination as a Baptist minister, his teaching and educational administrative duties in Alabama and Mississippi, and his church activities in Washington, D.C.

22. Bechet, Sidney (1897-1959). *Treat It Gentle*. Foreword by Desmond Fuller. Illustrated. Appendix. Index. New York: Hill & Wang, 1960. 245p.

   DHU   InU   MnU   MoU   NN   NcD   PLuL   PPiU   WU   WaU

   After summarizing his family background and his early life in New Orleans, Bechet reminisces about his music career, much of it in Europe, as a jazz soprano saxophonist.

23. Beck, Robert [under pseud. of Iceberg Slim] (1918-   ). *Pimp: The Story of My Life*. Glossary. Los Angeles: Holloway House, 1969. 317p.

   CSt   DLC   MiU   PPiU   WvU

   A reformed pimp and petty criminal who had operated in Milwaukee, Chicago, Detroit, Toledo, Cleveland, and Seattle, Beck vividly recounts the thrills and setbacks of his life. His narrative also describes his youth in Chicago, Indianapolis, Milwaukee, and Rockford, Illinois, as well as his prison experiences. [See Item 307.]

24. Blair, Norvel (b. 1825). *Life of Norvel Blair, a Negro Citizen of Morris, Grundy County, Illinois*. Joliet, Ill.: Joliet Daily Record Steam Print, 1880. 32p.

   NNC

   This pamphlet covers Blair's slave life in Tennessee and Arkansas, and his later endeavors as a farmer and property owner in Morris, Illinois. The author attempts to expose the deceptions allegedly employed by the local Republican Party to deprive him of his property and civil rights.

25. Brehan, Delle (1930-   ). *Kicks Is Kicks*. Los Angeles: Holloway House, 1970. 254p.

   PPiCl

   Known as the Black Queen of Pain, the author luridly details her career as a specialized sort of prostitute in New York City. She also explains the means by which she learned the psychological skills of her craft.

26. Brooks, Gwendolyn Elizabeth (1917-   ). *Report from Part One*. Prefaces by Don L. Lee and George Kent. Illustrated. Detroit: Broadside Press, 1972. 215p.

   DLC   PPi   PPiCl   PPiU

   Famous as a poet and novelist, Brooks provides a somewhat rambling account of her life and career. She was born in Topeka, Kansas, but was reared in Chicago, where she has spent most of her life. She also taught at Columbia College (Chicago), Elmhurst College, Northeastern Illinois State College, and the University of Wisconsin, and gave poetry readings and conducted poetry workshops in many cities and states. Included in her autobiography are interviews with the author and an impressionistic recollection of her visit to East Africa in 1971.

27. Broonzy, William Lee Conley (1898-1958). *Big Bill Blues: William Broonzy's Story*. As told to Yannick Bruynoghe. Foreword by Stanley Dance. Illustrated. Discography. Notes. Index. London: Cassell & Co., 1955. 139p.
    Reprinted New York: Oak Publications, 1964.
    CSdS CtHT DHU DLC FTaFA NN WvU
    This unchronological autobiography of the blues singer, musician, and composer rambles through his youth in Mississippi and Arkansas, his years as a sharecropper, his European military experiences during World War I, his work as a janitor at Iowa State College, and his music career in the U.S. and Europe.

28. Broughton, Virginia W. *Twenty Year's Experience of a Missionary*. Chicago: Pony Press, 1907. 140p.
    NN
    A Baptist evangelistic missionary, also active in the Woman's Christian Temperance Union, Broughton stresses her religious work. She was born free in Virginia, was graduated from Fisk University in 1875, and had a brief tenure as a school teacher and principal in Memphis before embarking on her missionary calling in the Midwest and South, working primarily in Tennessee. The autobiography is written in the third person.

29. Brown, Claude (1937-   ). *Manchild in the Promised Land*. New York: Macmillan, 1965. 415p.
    Reprinted New York: Signet Books—New American Library, 1966.
    CSdS CtHT DHU FTaFA NN OTU PLuL PPiCl PPiU WU
    Brown graphically portrays his youth and criminal activities in Harlem, his experiences in correctional institutions, and his personal struggle to redirect his life from crime toward law school.

30. Brown, H[ubert] Rap [Geroid] (1943-   ). *Die Nigger Die!* Illustrated. New York: Dial Press, 1969. 145p.
    CSdS CtHT CtY OkU PLuL PPiCl PPiU WU WaU WvU
    In this fiery, quasi-political autobiography, the author advocates revolutionary tactics to overcome white racism. He describes his youth in Louisiana, his college years at Southern University, and his political and civil rights activities, particularly those with the Student Nonviolent Coordinating Committee.

31. Brown, [James] Jimmy [Nathaniel] (1936-   ), with Myron Cope. *Off My Chest*. Foreword by Myron Cope. Illustrated. Index. Garden City, N.Y.: Doubleday, 1964. 230p.
    CtY DHU DLC ICU InU LU NN NjP PLuL PPi
    A former professional football player, later a film actor, focuses on his athletic career with the Cleveland Browns. He also depicts his youth in Georgia, his teen years on Long Island, and his collegiate life at Syracuse University, where he was also an outstanding lacrosse player.

32. Brown, Julia Clarice. *I Testify: My Years as an Undercover Agent for the FBI*. Introduction by Herbert Philbrick. Boston: Western Islands Publisher, 1966. 293p.

    DHU   DLC   NjP   WHi

    Concluding in an attack on the "Communist Conspiracy," this narrative by a Los Angeles housewife concentrates on her perilous life as an undercover agent in Cleveland for the U.S. Federal Bureau of Investigation from 1951 to 1960, after she had joined the Communist Party in 1947 and worked for civil rights organizations. Included are excerpts from testimonies by herself and others in 1962 before the U.S. Congressional House Committee on Un-American Activities. Brown touches as well on her earlier life in Atlanta and Detroit.

33. Brown, Lee—see Gonzales, Babs.

34. Brown, Sterling Nelson (1858-1929). *My Own Life Story*. Washington: Hamilton Printing Co., 1924. 47p.

    DHU

    A Congregational minister and professor at the Howard University School of Religion describes his slave life in Tennessee, his education at Fisk University and the Oberlin Theological Seminary, his religious work in Cleveland and Washington, D.C., and his teaching career.

35. Brown, William J. (1814-1885). *The Life of William J. Brown, of Providence, R.I.; with Personal Recollections of Incidents in Rhode Island*. Providence: Angell & Co., 1883. 230p.

    Reprinted Freeport, N.Y.: Books for Libraries Press, 1972.

    CtY   DHU   DLC   NN   NcD

    The quality and conditions of Negro life in Rhode Island are the focal points in this autobiography of a shoemaker and Baptist minister who was also active in civic organizations and the political life of Providence.

36. Browne, Rose Butler (1897-   ), and James English. *Love My Children: An Autobiography*. Index. New York: Meredith Press, 1969. 246p.

    CoU   FTaSU   ICU   KU   MB   MH   MoSW   NcU   PLuL   ViU

    A woman who taught at Virginia Normal and Technical Institute, Virginia State College, Bluefield (West Virginia) State College, West Virginia State College, and North Carolina College recounts her career, together with her youth in Boston and Newport, Rhode Island; her education at the Rhode Island Normal School, the University of Rhode Island, and Harvard University; and her work in the Baptist Church.

37. Bruce, H[enry] C[lay] (1836-1902). *The New Man. Twenty-Nine Years a Slave. Twenty-Nine Years a Free Man: Recollections of H. C. Bruce*. York, Pa.: P. Anstadt & Sons, 1895. 176p.

    Reprinted Miami, Fla.: Mnemosyne Publishing Co., 1969.

    Reprinted New York: Negro Universities Press, 1969.

DHU MH NSyU NcD OO PPiU PU TNF WHi WvU

The narrative of Bruce's slave life in Virginia, Mississippi, and Missouri is followed by an account of his experiences at odd jobs, his business ventures, and his duties with the U.S. Pension Office in Kansas.

38. Bruner, Peter (1845-1938). *A Slave's Adventures Toward Freedom; Not Fiction, but the True Story of a Struggle*. Illustrated. Oxford, Ohio: The Author, 1925. 54p.

KyBgW NN NjP OC OOxM

Having fought in the Union Army during the Civil War after a harsh slave life in Kentucky, Bruner migrated to Oxford, Ohio, where he was first a laborer and then a janitor and caretaker at Miami University.

39. Burton, Annie L. (b. 1858?). *Memories of Childhood's Slavery Days*. Boston: Ross Publishing Co., 1909. 97p.

DHU DLC MB NN

The narrative of the author's life as a slave in Alabama precedes her description of various jobs and business ventures in Macon and Atlanta, Georgia; Jacksonville, Florida; Newport, Rhode Island; and Boston. Burton's autobiography also includes some of her poems, reproductions of her favorite hymns, and an essay on racial matters by Dr. P. Thomas Stanford.

40. Burton, Thomas William (1860-1939). *What Experience Has Taught Me*. Introduction by John Wesley Gazaway. Illustrated. Cincinnati: Press of Jennings & Graham, 1910. 126p.

DHU DLC NN NcRR OCLloyd PP PLuL WHi

A physician in Springfield, Ohio, recalls his days in slavery in Kentucky, his education at Berea College and the Medical College of Indiana, and his career in medicine. Scattered through his autobiography are some of Dr. Burton's poems.

41. Campanella, Roy (1921-   ). *It's Good to Be Alive*. Illustrated. Boston: Little, Brown, 1959. 306p.

CtY DHU MiU NN NcD OrU PLuL PPi PSt WHi

A former professional baseball player with Negro teams and the Brooklyn Dodgers, later crippled in an automobile accident, describes his athletic career, his struggle to enter white baseball leagues, and his youth in Philadelphia.

42. Carnegie, Amos Hubert (1885-   ). *Faith Moves Mountains: An Autobiography*. Introduction by William Hallock Johnson. Washington: The Author, 1950. 114p.

DHU DLC NN NcSalL PLuL TxU

Born and reared in Jamaica, Carnegie sailed for Canada in 1913, where he was later imprisoned for refusing induction into military service during World War I. He participated in Baptist Church activities in Ontario before migrating to the U.S., where he attended Virginia

Union University and Lincoln University (Pennsylvania). He initiated a Sunday school mission and established schools in South Carolina, later becoming a minister in the African Methodist Episcopal Church and serving in Chattanooga. His autobiography highlights his successful efforts to build a high school in Marion, Virginia.

43. Carson, Robert "Sonny"—see Abubadika, Mwlina Imiri.

44. Cayton, Horace Roscoe (1903-1970). *Long Old Road*. New York: Trident Press, 1965. 402p.

    Reprinted Seattle: Univ. of Washington Press, 1970.

    CSdS CtH DHU FTaFA ICU NN PLuL PPiCl WHi WvU

    A prominent sociologist, scholar, and journalist reveals the private and often intensely painful story of his life, his search for racial and personal identity, and his struggles with alcoholism. He outlines at the same time his youth in Seattle, his activities as a seaman, his experiences in Alaska, his education at the University of Chicago, his work as a reporter at the United Nations, and his other professional pursuits.

45. Chisholm, Shirley (1924-   ). *Unbought and Unbossed*. Boston: Houghton Mifflin, 1970. 177p.

    Reprinted New York: Avon Books, 1971.

    CSt DHU NN NjR PPi PPiU WHi WU WvU

    The U.S. Democratic Congresswoman from New York City comments on a variety of political topics and racial issues, while recalling her youth in Brooklyn and on Barbados Island, her collegiate life at Brooklyn College, and her political career. [See Item 315.]

46. Christian, Malcolm Henry (1904-   ). *My Country and I: The Interracial Experiences of an American Negro, with Essays on Interracial Understanding*. New York: Exposition Press, 1963. 96p.

    DHU DLC FTaFA ICU NN NNC PPi WvU

    A highly articulate U.S. Postal Service worker in Chicago deals with his Ohio childhood, his education at Storer College and Howard University, his diversified occupations in Massachusetts and New York State, his travels in the U.S., and his life in Chicago after 1927. The last quarter of his book is a collection called "Essays on Interracial Understanding."

47. Clark, Septima Poinsette (1898-   ), with LeGette Blythe. *Echo in My Soul*. Foreword by Harry Golden. Illustrated. New York: Dutton, 1962. 243p.

    DHU DLC FTaFA NN NcSalL PPi WHi WvU

    Born, reared, and educated in South Carolina, where she was a school teacher for forty years, the author relates important experiences in her private and professional lives, including her participation in the racially integrated Highlander Folk School in Tennessee, an educational project sponsored by the Southern Christian Leadership Conference.

48. Clement, Samuel Spottford (b. 1861). *Memoirs of Samuel Spottford Clement: Relating Interesting Experiences in Days of Slavery and Freedom*. Steubenville, Ohio: Herald Printing Co., 1908. 67p.

    DLC

    A laborer, businessman, and constable in Steubenville, Ohio, remembers his childhood days as a slave in Virginia, his various jobs in the Lynchburg area and in West Virginia, and his Ohio years after 1883.

49. Clytus, John (1929-   ), with Jane Rieker. *Black Man in Red Cuba*. Coral Gables, Fla.: Univ. of Miami Press, 1970. 158p.

    AAP   CtY   KyU   MiU   NcU   OU   PPi   PPiU   WU   WaU

    Disillusioned by racial and political attitudes in the U.S., Clytus tried to emigrate to Africa in 1964, but stopped in Cuba, where he was detained for three years. Details of his unhappy Cuban experiences are punctuated with references to his early years in Oklahoma and San Francisco, his duties in the U.S. Air Force, his collegiate life at San Francisco State College, and his political campaign work for a Communist Party candidate in San Francisco.

50. Coles, Samuel B. (1888-1957). *Preacher with a Plow*. Illustrated. Boston: Houghton Mifflin, 1957. 241p.

    CtH   DHU   DLC   NN   PLuL   PPi

    An Alabama agricultural missionary for the Congregational Church chronicles his thirty-three years in Angola, Portuguese West Africa.

51. Cooke, W[ilson] C. *The Rungless Ladder: A Story of How Failures Led to Successful Living*. Illustrated. New York: Exposition Press, 1960. 49p.

    DHU   MoSW

    A self-styled minister and faith healer sketches his early life in Alabama, his education at Tuskegee Institute, his hospital work in Nashville, his real estate and business ventures in Chicago and Detroit, and his successful religious endeavors in Cleveland, where he founded and operated the Progressive Healing Center.

52. Coppin, Levi Jenkins (1848-1924). *Unwritten History*. Illustrated. Philadelphia: A.M.E. Book Concern, 1919. 375p.

    Reprinted New York: Negro Universities Press, 1968.

    DHU   FTaFA   MiU   NcRR   OWibfU   PLuL   PPiU   ViU   WHi   WvU

    An essayist, school teacher, and bishop in the African Methodist Episcopal Church focuses on his religious life and activities, especially in Baltimore, Philadelphia, and Wilmington, Delaware. He was born and reared in Maryland. [See Items 320 and 321.]

53. Corrothers, James David (1869-1917). *In Spite of the Handicap: An Autobiography*. Introduction by Ray Stannard Baker. Illustrated. New York: George H. Doran Co., 1916. 238p.

    Reprinted Westport, Conn.: Negro Universities Press, 1970.

    Reprinted Freeport, N.Y.: Books for Libraries Press, 1971.

DHU NN NcD NcU OCl PLuL PP PPiCl ViU WHi

Teacher, journalist, poet, and minister in both the Methodist Episco-pal and Baptist churches, Corrothers advocates "race progress" in the account of his early life in Michigan, jobs in the Midwest, his education at Northwestern University, his journalistic career on Chicago newspa-pers, his brief teaching tenure at Bennett College, and his ministerial work in many states, particularly New York, New Jersey, Michigan, Virginia, and Massachusetts.

54. Cotton, Ella Earls. *A Spark for My People: The Sociological Autobiog-raphy of a Negro Teacher*. New York: Exposition Press, 1954. 288p.

DHU GU MB NN OOxM PPi PSt PU TU WU

Born and reared in Virginia, a graduate of Knoxville College, the author was a school teacher in Alabama for most of her life.

55. Crumes, Cole, Sr. (1906-1968). *My Life Is an Open Book*. Illustrated. New York: Carlton Press, 1965. 80p.

DHU NN NcD

This rather fragmented autobiography covers the author's early life in Louisiana, his education at Prairie View State Industrial College (Texas) and Leland College (Louisiana), his U.S. Army experiences in North Africa and Italy during World War II, and his lengthy teaching career, begun in 1930, in Assumption Parish, Louisiana.

56. Dancy, John Campbell (1888-1967). *Sand Against the Wind: The Memoirs of John C. Dancy*. Foreword by Frank Angelo. Illustrated. Appendixes. Detroit: Wayne State Univ. Press, 1966. 249p.

CSdS DHU DLC FTaSU NcSalL NjR PLuL PPi PPiCl

For forty-two years the Director of the Detroit Urban League, Dancy concentrates on his community and civil rights activities, briefly taking into account his youth and adolescence in North Carolina, the North-east, and Washington, D.C.

57. Dandridge, Dorothy (1924-1965), and Earl Conrad. *Everything and Nothing: The Dorothy Dandridge Tragedy*. Foreword by Earl Conrad. Illustrated. New York: Abelard-Schuman, 1970. 215p.

Reprinted New York: Tower Publications, 1971.

CtH DHU DLC PPi PPiU WU

The life story of the popular singer and film actress embraces her personal as well as her professional life. Her early years were spent in Cleveland and Nashville, and then in touring the U.S. as a child actress and singer. Many of the episodes of her adult life occurred in the Los Angeles area.

58. Davidson, Henry Damon (b. 1869). *"Inching Along"; or the Life and Work of an Alabama Farm Boy: An Autobiography*. Introduction by H. Councill Trenholm. Illustrated. Nashville: National Publication Co., 1944. 177p.

DHU DLC NN NcD PLuL TxU ViU WHi

The founder and first principal of the Centreville (Alabama) Industrial Institute describes his early life as a farm boy in Alabama; his education at several institutions, including Payne University, Tuskegee Institute, Hampton Institute, Columbia University, and Fisk University; and his work as a teacher and administrator for the school he founded in 1900. The last half of his autobiography features a selection of his addresses and lectures.

59. Davis, Benjamin Jefferson (1903-1964). *Communist Councilman from Harlem: Autobiographical Notes Written in a Federal Penitentiary.* Introduction by Henry Winston. Illustrated. Appendix. New York: International Publishers, 1969. 218p.

   CSdS   PPiU   WU

   Written in the Federal prison at Terre Haute, Indiana, where the author was serving a five-year sentence under the Smith Act for his subversive activities, this narrative describes Davis's early life in Georgia, his involvement as a lawyer in numerous controversial court cases and labor organizational efforts, his three terms as a Communist on the New York City Council, and his trial and imprisonment.

60. Davis, Sammy, Jr. (1925-   ), with Jane and Burt Boyar. *Yes I Can: The Story of Sammy Davis, Jr.* Illustrated. New York: Farrar, Straus, & Giroux, 1965. 612p.

   Reprinted New York: Pocket Books, 1966.

   CtH   DHU   FTaFA   NN   NcSalL   PLuL   PPiCl   PPiU   WHi   WU

   The popular singer, dancer, actor, and comedian vividly and frankly details his private and professional life, beginning with his childhood in Harlem.

61. Day, Helen Caldwell (1926-   ). *Color, Ebony.* New York: Sheed & Ward, 1951. 182p.

   CSdS   DHU   DLC   IaU   MB   MiU   PLuL   PPi   ViU   WHi

   Confined to a tuberculosis sanatorium, the author focuses on her conversion from Methodism to Roman Catholicism and her charitable work as a Catholic volunteer in Memphis. She writes also of her youth in Texas, her training as a nurse in Brooklyn, her various jobs in Iowa and Mississippi, her Cadet Student Nurse accomplishments in Harlem during World War II, and her stint as a writer for a Memphis newspaper. [See next item.]

62. Day, Helen Caldwell (1926-   ). *Not Without Tears.* New York: Sheed & Ward, 1954. 270p.

   DHU   DLC   NN   NcD   NcRR   PP   PPi   ViU   WHi

   As a practical nurse and volunteer organizer among Catholic and interracial groups in Memphis, Day continues the memoirs begun in her first autobiography. [See preceding item.]

63. Dean, Harry (b. 1864), with Sterling North. *The Pedro Gorino: The Adventures of a Negro Sea-Captain in Africa and on the Seven Seas in*

His Attempts to Found an Ethiopian Empire: An Autobiographical Narrative. Preface by Sterling North. Boston: Houghton Mifflin, 1929. 262p.

DHU DLC FTaSU MB MiU NN NcD PPiU OrU TxU

The subtitle of this autobiography accurately commemorates Dean's purpose through fifty years on his schooner, the *Pedro Gorino*. Before he tells of his adventures on the seas, in Africa, and on other continents, the author mentions his early life in Philadelphia.

64. Delaney, Lucy A. Berry (b. 1828?). *From Darkness Cometh the Light; or, Struggles for Freedom*. St. Louis: Publishing House of J. T. Smith, 1891. 64p.

DHU MH MiU OCl OClWHi WHi

Active in Negro civic and social organizations in St. Louis, Delaney recalls also her slave life there, the court case through which she won her freedom in 1844, and her life in Quincy, Illinois.

65. Donaldson, Allen—see Jamal, Hakim Abdullah.

66. Douglass, Frederick (1817-1895). *Life and Times of Frederick Douglass, Written by Himself: His Early Life as a Slave, His Escape from Bondage, and His Complete History to the Present Time*. Introduction by George L. Ruffin. Illustrated. Appendix. Hartford, Conn.: Park Publishing Co., 1881. 518p.

Revised and reprinted Boston: DeWolfe, Fiske & Co., 1892.
Reprinted New York: Pathway Press, 1941.
Reprinted New York: Collier Books, 1962.
Abridged and reprinted New York: Thomas Y. Crowell, 1966.
Abridged and reprinted New York: Grosset & Dunlap, 1970.

DHU DLC FTaFA NN NcD PP PLuL PPi PPiCl WHi

The famous former slave and abolitionist writes of his years of bondage in Maryland, his escape to Massachusetts in 1838, his oratories in the Northeast and Midwest for the Anti-Slavery Society, his travels and talks in the British Isles, and his editorship and publication of *The North Star* from Rochester, New York. He also tells of his civil rights activities after the Civil War, his work for the Freedman's Bank, his participation on the Commission to Santo Domingo, and his duties for the Federal Government in Washington, D.C. The 1892 edition of his autobiography adds reports of his European and Middle Eastern journeys of 1886-1887, and of his responsibilities as minister to Haiti from 1889. [See Items 432 and 433.]

67. Du Bois, William Edward Burghardt (1868-1963). *The Autobiography of W. E. B. Du Bois: A Soliloquy on Viewing My Life from the Last Decade of Its First Century*. Edited and Preface by Herbert Aptheker. Notes. Bibliography. Index. New York: International Publishers, 1968. 448p.

AU CtY DHU KyU NcD OrU PPiCl PPiU ViU WaU

The civil rights leader, also a sociologist, essayist, editor, fiction writer, poet, and teacher, begins his autobiography with his childhood in Great Barrington, Massachusetts, and concludes it as a citizen of Ghana, to which he emigrated after he had joined the Communist Party in 1961. Educated at Fisk University, Harvard University, and the University of Berlin, he taught at Wilberforce University, the University of Pennsylvania, and Atlanta University. He was the founder and editor of both *The Crisis* and *Phylon*, and was a leading figure in the NAACP. His autobiography also describes his many trips to Europe, Africa, and Asia and his efforts for international cooperation and world peace. [See Items 324, 325, and 326.]

68. Dunham, Katherine (1910-   ). *A Touch of Innocence*. New York: Harcourt, Brace & World, 1959. 312p.

CtH   DHU   DLC   FTaFA   NN   PLuL   PPi   PPiU   WHi   WU

The dancer, choreographer, and anthropologist narrates the first eighteen years of her life in the third person, years spent on an Illinois farm, and in Chicago, Joliet, and Glen Ellyn, Illinois. [See Items 327 and 328.]

69. Edwards, William James (1869-1950). *Twenty-Five Years in the Black Belt*. Illustrated. Appendix. Boston: Cornhill Co., 1918. 143p.

Reprinted Westport, Conn.: Negro Universities Press, 1970.

AU   CtHT   DHU   FTaFA   MiU   NN   NcD   PLuL   PPiU   ViU

The founder of the Snow Hill (Alabama) Institute treats his youth in Alabama, his education at Tuskegee Institute, and his achievements at Snow Hill. Part of his book is a history of the Institute and a collection of his essays on racial problems.

70. Everett, Syble Ethel Byrd (1902?-   ). *Adventures with Life: An Autobiography of a Distinguished Negro Citizen*. Introduction and Epilogue by Faye P. Everett. Illustrated. Boston: Meador Publishing Co., 1945. 182p.

DHU   DLC   NN   NcD   PPi   ViHaI   WHi

A teacher in Oklahoma schools, at Langston University, and at the School of Related Arts in St. Louis recalls her early life in Oklahoma, her education at Langston University and the University of Utah, her teaching career, and her activities in the African Methodist Episcopal Church. Some chapters outline her personal philosophy and include many of her poems.

71. Evers, Charles (1922-   ). *Evers*. Edited and Introduction by Grace Halsell. Cleveland: World Publishing Co., 1971. 196p.

CtH   LN   MiEM   PPi   PPiCl   PPiU   RP   WU   Wa   WvU

The mayor of Fayette, Mississippi, and the brother of assassinated civil rights leader Medgar Evers deals with his early life in Mississippi, his military service in the Pacific with the U.S. Army during World

War II, his jobs and criminal activities in Chicago, and his civil rights
work and political career in Mississippi.

72. Ferebee, London R. (b. 1849). *A Brief History of the Slave Life of
Rev. L. R. Ferebee, and the Battles of Life, and Four Years of His
Ministerial Life*. Raleigh, N.C.: Edwards, Broughton & Co., 1882. 24p.
   Nc   NcU
   The North Carolina resident summarily narrates his slave life, his
   tenure as a teacher, his ministerial work in the African Methodist
   Episcopal Church, and his activities for the Republican Party. He
   attempts also to refute the charges which led to his brief imprison-
   ment.

73. Ferguson, Ira Lunan (1904-   ). *I Dug Graves at Night to Attend College by Day: The Story of a West Indian Negro-American's First 30
Years in the United States: An Autobiography*. Vol. 1. Illustrated.
Brooklyn: Theo. Gaus' Sons, 1968. 486p.
   CU   IU   InU   MiU   MsU   NjP   NIC   NNC   PPiCl   TU
   A San Francisco psychologist who is also an essayist and novelist
   devotes about half of this volume of his autobiography to his experiences during the 1920s as a traveling stenographer and business assist-
   ant to a man operating from Mifflinburg, Pennsylvania. Ferguson
   earlier describes his youth in Jamaica and his brief residence in Philadelphia. Later, he accounts for his education at Howard University,
   the University of Minnesota, and Columbia University. He worked at
   numerous jobs, including grave digging, to finance his education, and
   held minor positions in the U.S. Government. In addition, he taught at
   Southern University. This volume covers his life to 1950. [See next
   item and Items 330a and 331.]

74. Ferguson, Ira Lunan (1904-   ). *I Dug Graves at Night to Attend Col-
lege by Day: My Later Years as a Naturalized West Indian-American:
An Autobiography*. Vol. 2. Prologue by Nelson L. Bossing, Henry M.
Ladrey, Maurice M. Gordon, and Jay Arthur Myers. Illustrated. San
Francisco: Lunan-Ferguson Library, 1969. 492p.
   CU   DLC   InU   KyU   MiU   NN   NNC   NjP   PPiCl   PPiU
   Referring to his later activities as a psychologist, essayist, and novelist, Ferguson picks up his narrative during his graduate years at
   Columbia University, which awarded him a Ph.D. in 1950. He taught
   at Tuskegee Institute and San Diego Junior College before he began
   practicing as a psychologist in San Francisco in 1957. He also mentions
   his work for civic organizations and for the Republican Party. [See
   preceding item and Items 330a and 331.]

75. Ferris, Louanne [pseud.] (1925-   ). *I'm Done Crying*. As told to Beth
Day. Foreword by Beth Day. New York: M. Evans & Co., 1969. 275p.
   Reprinted New York: Signet Books—New American Library, 1970.

CtH   DHU   DLC   NN   PPi
This graphic account of the author's experiences as a nurse in a
metropolitan hospital (probably in New York City) also alludes to
her early years in Alabama.

76.   Flipper, Henry Ossian (1856-1940). *The Colored Cadet at West Point:
Autobiography of Lieut. Henry Ossian Flipper, U.S.A., First Graduate
of Color from the U.S. Military Academy*. New York: Homer Lee &
Co., 1878. 322p.
     Reprinted New York: Arno Press, 1969.
     Reprinted New York: Johnson Reprint Corp., 1969.
     CSdS   DHU   FTaFA   MB   NN   NSyU   PLuL   PPiU   ViU   WHi
     Primarily covering his life at West Point from 1873 to 1877, Flipper
documents his book with newspaper articles, official and private letters, and speeches by military personnel. He was born in Georgia and
grew up in Atlanta. [See next item.]

77.   Flipper, Henry Ossian (1856-1940). *Negro Frontiersman: The Western
Memoirs of Henry O. Flipper, First Negro Graduate of West Point*.
Edited and Introduction by Theodore D. Harris. Notes. El Paso: Texas
Western College Press, 1963. 54p.
     DLC   FTaFA   NN   TxU   WHi
     These memoirs were written when Flipper served as a U.S. Army
Cavalry officer in the Southwest from 1878 to 1882, and while he was
a civil and mining engineer in the Southwest and Mexico from 1882 to
1916. [See preceding item.]

78.   Flood, [Curtis] Curt Charles (1938-   ), with Richard Carter. *The Way
It Is*. Appendixes. New York: Trident Press, 1971. 236p.
     Reprinted New York: Pocket Books, 1972.
     CtH   IU   IaU   InU   MB   MeB   NjP   PPi   ViU   WHi
     While describing and defending his legal suit against professional base-
ball's "reserve clause," which binds a player to his team, Flood also
tells of his youth in Houston and Oakland and recounts his experiences
as a player for the St. Louis Cardinals.

79.   Foote, Julia A. J. (b. 1823). *A Brand Plucked from the Fire: An Autobiographical Sketch*. Introduction by Thomas K. Doty. Cleveland: The
Author, 1879. 124p.
     Reprinted New York: G. Hughes & Co., 1879.
     DHU   DLC   MH   NN   OCl   TNF   WHi
     An African Methodist Episcopal evangelist preacher who grew up in
Schenectady and Albany, New York, focuses on her religious vocation
and travels in the Northeast and Canada. She was called into the religious life following a mystical experience in Boston.

80.   Forman, James (1928-   ). *The Making of Black Revolutionaries: A
Personal Account*. Index. New York: Macmillan, 1972. 568p.
     CtH   DLC   PPi   PPiCl   PPiU   WvU

The civil rights leader and political activist concentrates on his often dangerous activities during the 1960s, particularly with the Freedom Riders and the Student Nonviolent Coordinating Committee, and briefly with the Black Panther Party. He also portrays his early life in Chicago and Mississippi; his duties in the U.S. Air Force, especially on Okinawa; his education at the University of Southern California, Roosevelt University, Boston University, the University of Chicago, and Middlebury College; his life as a teacher in Chicago; his jail experiences; and his visits to Africa.

81. Foster, [George] Pops [Murphy] (1892-1969). *Pops Foster: The Autobiography of a New Orleans Jazzman*. As told to, and Foreword by, Tom Stoddard. Introduction by Bertram Turetzky. Interchapters by Ross Russell. Illustrated. Discography by Brian Rust. Index. Berkeley: Univ. of California Press, 1971. 208p.

    CU   DLC   PPiCl   WU

    Born in Louisiana and reared in New Orleans from the age of ten, Foster recalls his career as a jazz bass player in New Orleans, Los Angeles, St. Louis, New York City, San Francisco, and smaller cities throughout the country, as well as on Mississippi River steamboats.

82. Frazier, Walt (1945-   ), and Joe Jares. *Clyde*. Illustrated. New York: Rutledge Books—Holt, Rinehart & Winston, 1970. 286p.

    Reprinted New York: Grosset & Dunlap, 1971.

    CtH   DLC   PPi   WHi

    A basketball player concentrates on his athletic career as a youth in Atlanta, a student at Southern Illinois University, and a professional for the New York Knickerbockers.

83. Frederick, Francis (b. 1809). *Autobiography of Rev. Francis Frederick, of Virginia*. Baltimore: J. W. Woods, Printer, 1869. 40p.

    DLC   OCl   OClWHi   OOxM   PPL   PPPrHi   WHi   WvU

    A Baltimore colporteur and Presbyterian minister, Frederick primarily narrates his slave life in Virginia and Kentucky, his escape to Canada in 1855, and his travels in the British Isles.

84. Fuller, Thomas Oscar (1867-1942). *Twenty Years in Public Life, 1890-1910*. Illustrated. Nashville: National Baptist Publication Board, 1910. 279p.

    DLC   WHi

    A teacher and Baptist minister, born and reared in North Carolina and educated at Shaw University, Fuller provides a lengthy account of his terms as a Republican member of the North Carolina Senate in 1898 and 1899. He taught at and was then principal of Shiloh Institute, later assuming ministerial duties in Memphis and the principalship of Howe Institute there. His autobiography contains a selection of his sermons, addresses, and essays.

85. Gaudet, Frances Joseph (1861-1934). *"He Leadeth Me."* New Orleans: The Author, 1913. 144p.

    LNHT   TxU

    President of the Woman's Christian Temperance Union of Louisiana and founder of the Colored Industrial Home and School Association in New Orleans for homeless children, Gaudet also pioneered for prison reform in Louisiana. Her story encompasses her childhood in Mississippi, and features a lengthy account of her trip to the British Isles and France.

86. Gibbs, Mifflin Wistar (1823-1918). *Shadow and Light: An Autobiography, with Reminiscences of the Last and Present Century*. Introduction by Booker T. Washington. Illustrated. Washington: The Author, 1902. 372p.

    Reprinted New York: Arno Press, 1968.

    CSdS DHU NN OTU PLuL PPi PPiU ViHaI WHi WvU

    A man who eventually became a lawyer in Arkansas and was appointed U.S. consul to Madagascar traces his life through these events and his youth in Philadelphia, his civil rights accomplishments in California, his business ventures in Canada, and his judgeship position in Little Rock, Arkansas.

87. Gibson, Althea (1927-   ). *I Always Wanted to Be Somebody*. Edited by Edward E. Fitzgerald. Illustrated. New York: Harper & Bros., 1958. 176p.

    Reprinted New York: Perennial Library—Harper & Row, 1965.

    Reprinted New York: Falcon Books—Noble & Noble, 1967.

    CSt CtY DHU FTaFA MiU NN NcD PLuL PPi WHi

    The world champion tennis player describes her career, together with her young years in South Carolina, Harlem, and Wilmington, Delaware, and her student days at Florida Agricultural and Mechanical College. [See next item.]

88. Gibson, Althea (1927-   ), with Richard Curtis. *So Much to Live For.* Introduction by Richard Curtis. Index. New York: Putnam's, 1968. 160p.

    DLC   PLuL   PPi

    In a book for young readers, the world champion tennis player continues the story of her athletic career, including her experiences as a professional golfer. [See preceding item.]

89. Gibson, [Robert] Bob (1935-   ), with Phil Pepe. *From Ghetto to Glory: The Story of Bob Gibson*. Illustrated. Englewood Cliffs, N.J.: Prentice-Hall, 1968. 200p.

    Reprinted New York: Popular Library, 1968.

    DLC   NN   PLuL   PPi

    A pitcher for the St. Louis Cardinals writes not only about his baseball career, but also about his youth in Omaha, his collegiate activities

at Creighton University, and his basketball feats for the Harlem Globe-
trotters.

90. Gonzales, Babs [formerly Brown, Lee] (1926-   ). *I Paid My Dues:
Good Times . . . No Bread*. East Orange, N.J.: Expubidence Publishing
Corp., 1967. 160p.
    Revised and reprinted New York: Lancer Books, 1971.
    DHU
    Accounts from both his private and his professional life appear in
this autobiography of a musician, singer, and band leader. He covers
his experiences during his youth in Newark, New Jersey, and on his
travels and performances in the U.S., Canada, and Europe. The revised
edition continues the author's adventures after 1967.

91. Goodwin, Ruby Berkley (1903-   ). *It's Good to Be Black*. Garden
City, N.Y.: Doubleday, 1953. 256p.
    AU   DHU   FTaFA   MB   NN   PLuL   PPi   PPiU   PSt   WHi
    A fiction writer, poet, and author of children's stories reminisces
about her happy childhood and adolescence in the coal-mining town
of Du Quoin, Illinois.

92. Gordon, Taylor (1893-1970). *Born to Be*. Foreword by Muriel Draper.
Introduction by Carl Van Vechten. Illustrated. Glossary. New York:
Covici-Friede, 1929. 236p.
    CoU   GU   IU   IaU   NN   NcD   NjP   OrU   PPiU   ViHaI
    A gospel singer who achieved prominence in the U.S. and Europe
describes his childhood in Montana, his occupations in Minnesota, his
work on railroad passenger trains in the Northwest, his employment as
a chauffeur for the Ringling family of circus fame, and the beginning
of his singing career.

93. Grant, Daniel T. (1914-   ). *When the Melon Is Ripe: The Autobiography of a Georgia Negro High School Principal and Minister*. Appendixes. New York: Exposition Press, 1955. 174p.
    DHU   DLC   FTaFA   NN   NcD   NcRR   PLuL   PP   WHi   WvU
    Born and reared in Georgia, educated at Morris Brown College, Atlan-
ta University, Ohio State University, and Capital University, this
Georgia high school principal emphasizes both the difficulties he en-
countered in an earlier principalship and the mysterious attempts to
force him into participating in Communist Party activities. He also
briefly mentions his vocations as an African Methodist Episcopal minister, a concert pianist, and a high school band director.

94. Grant, Robert Lee (1938-   ), with Carl Gardner. *The Star Spangled
Hustle*. Philadelphia: Lippincott, 1972. 240p.
    DLC   PPiCl   PPiU
    An economist focuses on his years in Sweden, where he earned his
Ph.D. from the University of Stockholm, and on his duties as an offi-
cial in the U.S. Department of Housing and Urban Development, a

position he was later removed from apparently through the direct
order of President Richard M. Nixon. Grant also alludes to his childhood in Hempstead, Long Island, his "hustling" and petty criminal
activities, and his collegiate life at Adelphi College and Queens College.

95. Green, Elisha Winfield (b. 1818?). *Life of the Rev. Elisha W. Green,
One of the Founders of the Kentucky Normal and Theological Institute—Now the State University of Louisville; Eleven Years Moderator
of the Mt. Zion Baptist Association; Five Years Moderator of the Con-
solidated Baptist Educational Association and Over Thirty Years Pastor
of the Colored Baptist Churches of Maysville and Paris*. Maysville, Ky.:
Republican Printing Office, 1888. 60p.

Reprinted, microcard, Louisville: Lost Cause Press, 1963.

DLC   MoU   NN   NcWsW   WvU

The author covers his years as a slave in Kentucky, his numerous
activities and accomplishments on behalf of the Baptist Church, the
duties of his pastorship in Maysville and Paris, Kentucky, and his
efforts to found the Kentucky Normal and Theological Institute.

96. Green, [Elisha] Ely (1893-1968). *Ely: An Autobiography*. Introduction by Lilian Smith. New York: Seabury Press, 1966. 236p.

DLC   PLuL   PPi   PPiU   WHi   WU

In an often ungrammatical but lively and colorful fashion, Green narrates his first eighteen years in Sewanee, Tennessee. [See next item.]

97. Green, [Elisha] Ely (1893-1968). *Ely: Too Black, Too White*. Edited
by Elizabeth N. and Arthur Ben Chitty. Foreword by Arthur Ben
Chitty. Amherst, Mass.: Univ. of Massachusetts Press, 1970. 637p.

Abridged and reprinted New York: Mentor Books—New American
Library, 1971.

CtHT   GU   ICU   InU   NcU   PPiCl   PPiU   ViU   WaU   WvU

Later a laborer at odd jobs and a private advocate of expanded civil
rights, Green first retells the story of his early life in Tennessee, then
continues to an account of his adventures in Texas, in Europe with the
U.S. Army during World War I, and in California. [See preceding item.]

98. Green, John Paterson (1845-1940). *Fact Stranger Than Fiction:
Seventy-Five Years of a Busy Life, with Reminiscences of Many Great
and Good Men and Women*. Illustrated. Index. Cleveland: Riehl Printing Co., 1920. 368p.

CtY   DHU   NN   NNC   NcD   NcU   OCl   OClWHi   PPPD   TNF

A lawyer, businessman, and politician, Green was born free and
reared in South Carolina. He moved to Cleveland in 1857, attended
Union Law School, and later served as a Republican in the Ohio State
Legislature. He was also a Justice of the Peace in Cleveland and was
appointed a minor official in the U.S. Post Office Department. His
autobiography includes memories of his three trips to Europe. [See
Item 339.]

99. Gregory, [Richard] Dick [Claxton] (1932-   ), with Robert Lipsyte. *Nigger: An Autobiography*. Illustrated. New York: Dutton, 1964. 224p.

Reprinted New York: Pocket Books, 1965.

CSdS CtHT DHU FTaSU NN PLuL PPi PPiCl WU WvU

A comedian, essayist, civil rights leader, and independent politician recalls his early life in St. Louis, his college years at Southern Illinois University including his exploits as a track star, his career in entertainment, and his civil rights activities. [See Item 340.]

100. Grimes, William W. (b. 1824). *Thirty-Three Years' Experience of an Itinerant Minister of the A.M.E. Church*. Lancaster, Pa.: E. S. Speaker, 1887. 30p.

TNF

In this pamphlet the author sketches his youth in and around Alexandria, Virginia, where he was born free, his experiences during two years in the U.S. Navy, his duties as a domestic servant in Washington, D.C., and his work as a minister in the African Methodist Episcopal Church. He preached in Delaware and Maryland before the Civil War, and later in New England and the Lancaster, Pennsylvania, area.

101. Guffy, Ossie (1931-   ). *Ossie: The Autobiography of a Black Woman*. As told to, and Preface by, Caryl Ledner. New York: Norton, 1971. 224p.

Reprinted New York: Bantam Books, 1972.

CtH DLC PPi PPiU WHi WU WvU

Labeling herself an "average" black woman, "one of the millions who ain't bright, militant, or talented," Guffy depicts her early life in the Cincinnati area and her experiences after 1960 in the Los Angeles area, where she often received welfare subsidies.

102. Handy, W[illiam] C[hristopher] (1873-1958). *Father of the Blues: An Autobiography*. Edited by Arna Bontemps. Foreword by Abbe Niles. Illustrated. Musical scores. Appendix. Index. New York: Macmillan, 1941. 317p.

Reprinted New York: Collier Books, 1970.

AAP CtH DHU FTaFA MB OrU PLuL PPiU WU WvU

The blues composer, musician, band leader, and owner of a music publishing company writes of his early life in Alabama, his adventures with traveling minstrel shows, his rise to prominence in Memphis, and his later music career and business venture in New York City.

103. Harrison, [Robert] Bob [Emanuel] (1928-   ), with James Montgomery. *When God Was Black*. Grand Rapids, Mich.: Zondervan Publishing House, 1971. 160p.

DLC PPiCl

An evangelical minister and religious singer, ordained in the

Assemblies of God Church, Harrison portrays his youth in San Francisco, his military service in the U.S. Army, his adventures as a jazz musician, his education at San Francisco State College, his training at Bethany Bible College (Santa Cruz, California), and his religious work. He pastored a church in San Francisco, later was a member of the Billy Graham Crusades, and made evangelical tours of Europe, Africa, and Asia.

104.   Heard, William Henry (1850-1937). *From Slavery to the Bishopric in the A.M.E. Church: An Autobiography*. Introduction by H. H. Cooper. Illustrated. Philadelphia: A.M.E. Book Concern, 1924. 104p.

   Reprinted New York: Arno Press, 1969.

   DHU   NN   NSyU   NcD   NjP   OU   PPiU   TNF   ViHaI   WU

   Heard was born a slave in Georgia. He later became a South Carolina legislator, the minister-resident and consul general to Liberia, and a bishop in the African Methodist Episcopal Church from 1908, after serving as a minister in South Carolina and Philadelphia.

105.   Hedgeman, Anna Arnold (1899-   ). *The Trumpet Sounds: A Memoir of Negro Leadership*. New York: Holt, Rinehart & Winston, 1964. 202p.

   CtH   DHU   DLC   FTaFA   FTaSU   NjR   PLuL   PPiU   WHi   WU

   Reared in a small town in Minnesota and educated at Rust College and Hamline University, the author recalls her youth and describes her varied careers, as a teacher, an official in the YWCA, an administrator for the U.S. Government, and a political and civil rights leader. She also reminisces about her trips to Europe and Africa.

106.   Henry, George (b. 1819). *Life of George Henry; Together with a Brief History of the Colored People of America*. N.P. [Providence?] : The Author, 1894. 123p.

   Reprinted Freeport, N.Y.: Books for Libraries Press, 1971.

   DLC   NB   NcSalL   PPiU   TNF

   A former Virginia slave who captained timber ships along the Atlantic coast writes of his sailing adventures, his escape to Philadelphia, and his maritime, business, and civil rights activities in Providence.

107.   Henson, Josiah (1789-1883). *"Uncle Tom's Story of His Life": An Autobiography of the Rev. Josiah Henson (Mrs. Harriet Beecher Stowe's "Uncle Tom")*. *From 1789 to 1876*. Edited and Editorial Note by John Lobb. Preface by Harriet Beecher Stowe. Introduction by George Sturge and S. Morley. Notes. Appendix. Index. Advertisements. London: "Christian Age" Office, 1876. 231p.

   Reprinted as *"Truth Is Stranger Than Fiction": An Autobiography of the Rev. Josiah Henson (Mrs. Harriet Beecher Stowe's "Uncle Tom")*, *from 1789-1879*. Boston: B. B. Russell & Co., 1879.

   Reprinted London: Frank Cass & Co., 1971.

   CU   FTaSU   N   NN   NjP   PPiU   TNF   TxU   ViU   WvU

Allegedly the prototype for Harriet Beecher Stowe's fictional "Uncle Tom," Henson was a slave in Maryland and Kentucky before his escape to Canada in 1830. He spent much of his later life as a Canadian timber farmer and sawmill owner, and a Methodist Episcopal minister. He also led escaping slaves out of Kentucky into Canada, and traveled several times to England, where he preached and orated. [See Item 439.]

108. Henson, Matthew Alexander (1866-1955). *A Negro Explorer at the North Pole*. Foreword by Robert E. Peary. Introduction by Booker T. Washington. Illustrated. Glossary. New York: F. A. Stokes, 1912. 200p.

Reprinted New York: Arno Press, 1969.

Reprinted as *A Black Explorer at the North Pole: An Autobiographical Report by the Negro Who Conquered the Top of the World with Admiral Robert E. Peary*. New York: Walker, 1969.

CSdS CtY DHU FTaFA NN NSyU PLuL PPiCl TxU WvU

His book features detailed coverage of his important participation in Admiral Peary's successful expedition to the North Pole, 1908-1909. Henson also depicts his early life in Maryland and Washington, D.C., and his adventures as a seaman.

109. Herndon, Angelo (1913-   ). *Let Me Live*. Illustrated. Appendixes. New York: Random House, 1937. 409p.

Reprinted New York: Arno Press, 1969.

CSdS CoU CtY IU OrU PLuL PPiU ViHaI WHi WvU

The controversial court cases in the 1930s over Herndon's indictment for allegedly attempting to incite an insurrection are the focal points in this autobiography. Also recounted are his youth in Ohio, his work as a coal miner and labor organizer in Alabama, his activities for the Communist Party in Alabama and Georgia, and his prison years.

110. Hicks, Estelle Bell (1891-1971). *The Golden Apples: Memoirs of a Retired Teacher*. New York: Exposition Press, 1959. 75p.

CtY DHU DLC NN NNC OU

A former science teacher, retired from the Mobile, Alabama, public school system in 1957, the author reminisces about her life in and out of the classroom.

111. Himes, Chester (1909-   ). *The Quality of Hurt: The Autobiography of Chester Himes*. Vol. 1. Garden City, N.Y.: Doubleday, 1972. 351p.

CtH DLC PPi PPiCl PPiU WU WvU

The noted novelist, born in Jefferson City, Missouri, treats his youth in Mississippi, Arkansas, St. Louis, and Cleveland, his student days at Ohio State University, his criminal activities in Cleveland and Chicago, his seven years in the Ohio State Penitentiary, his employment at various jobs in California and the New York City area, and his early

career as a fiction writer. The last half of this volume describes Himes'
life as an expatriate in Europe during 1953 and 1954.

112. Holiday,[Eleonora]Billie (1915-1959), with William Dufty. *Lady Sings
the Blues.* Discography. Garden City, N.Y.: Doubleday, 1956. 250p.
  Reprinted New York: Popular Library, 1958.
  Reprinted New York: Lancer Books, 1965.
  CtY   DHU   DLC   FTaFA   IU   MiU   NN   PPi   PPiU   TxU
  The popular singer depicts her youth in Baltimore and New York
City, her criminal activities, her experiences in correctional institutions
and prisons, her music career, and her battles against drug addiction.

113. Holley, Joseph Winthrop (1874-1958). *You Can't Build a Chimney
from the Top: The South Through the Life of a Negro Educator.*
Introduction by Chase S. and Stellanova Osborn. Illustrated. New
York: William-Frederick Press, 1948. 226p.
  DHU   DLC   FTaFA   NN   PLuL   PPi   TU   ViHaI   ViU   WHi
  A teacher, Presbyterian minister, and founder and first president of
Albany (Georgia) State College also portrays his childhood in South
Carolina and his education at Phillips Academy (Andover, Massachu-
setts) and Lincoln University (Pennsylvania).

114. Holtzclaw, William Henry (1870?-1943). *The Black Man's Burden.*
Introduction by Booker T. Washington. Illustrated. New York: Neale
Publishing Co., 1915. 232p.
  Reprinted New York: Haskell House, 1970.
  Reprinted New York: Negro Universities Press, 1970.
  DHU   MiU   NcD   OrU   PLuL   PPiU   TNF   ViHaI   WHi   WvU
  A teacher and the founder and first principal of the Utica (Missis-
sippi) Normal and Industrial Institute focuses on his struggles to build
and sustain his school, while also describing his youth in Alabama and
his education at Tuskegee Institute.

115. Horne, Lena (1917-   ). *In Person: Lena Horne.* As told to Helen
Arstein and Carlton Moss. Illustrated. New York: Greenberg Publisher, 1950. 249p.
  CtH   DHU   DLC   FTaFA   NN   PPi   ViHaI   WaU
  The popular singer and actress depicts her personal life and her
careers, especially in New York City, Pittsburgh, and Hollywood. [See
next item.]

116. Horne, Lena (1917-   ), and Richard Schickel. *Lena.* Illustrated.
Garden City, N.Y.: Doubleday, 1965. 300p.
  Reprinted New York: Signet Books—New American Library, 1966.
  CtHT   DHU   FTaFA   NN   NcSalL   NjP   PLuL   PPi   PPiCl   WU
  Continuing the story of her life and careers, the singer and actress
also reinterprets many aspects of her first autobiography. [See pre-
ceding item.]

117. Houston, Ruby R. (1908-   ). *I Was Afraid to Be Happy.* New York:

Carlton Press, 1967. 48p.

DHU   IEdS   IU   InU   MB   NjP

Candidly discussing her problems in romances and marriages, and her poverty, the author briefly describes her life in rural Tennessee, Chicago, and Memphis.

118. Howell, [Dressler] Jinxy Red [LaMarr] (1930-   ). *All the Hairs on My Head Hurt*. New York: Exposition Press, 1964. 197p.

DHU   DLC   IU   NN

A California dentist weaves a fascinating tale of the apparent mental disorders plaguing him while he was a dental surgeon in the U.S. Air Force, his experiences in mental institutions, the ensuing disruptions to his marriage and family, his attempts at suicide, and his successful recovery after the source of his illness was found to be a physical one. He alludes also to his early life in Greensboro, North Carolina, and to his education at Howard University.

119. Hudson, Hosea (1898-   ). *Black Worker in the Deep South: A Personal Record*. Introduction by Ralph David Abernathy. New York: International Publishers, 1972. 130p.

DLC   PPi   PPiCl   PPiU

Hudson writes of his life as a sharecrop farmer in rural Georgia, before he moved to Atlanta in 1923. He continues to accounts of his various jobs in Birmingham, Alabama, his work for the Communist Party, his labor organizing efforts, and his civil rights activities there until 1948. He then went to Newark, New Jersey, and worked in New York City. His autobiography stops in the early 1950s.

120. Hughes, Langston (1902-1967). *The Big Sea: An Autobiography*. New York: Knopf, 1940. 335p.

Reprinted New York: Hill & Wang, 1963.

AU   CSdS   DHU   FTaFA   NcD   OrU   PLuL   PPiU   WU   WvU

Covering his life to the end of the 1920s, the famous poet, dramatist, fiction writer, and essayist describes his youth in Kansas, Ohio, and Mexico, his global wanderings as a seaman, and his participation in the Harlem Renaissance cultural and literary movement. [See next item.]

121. Hughes, Langston (1902-1967). *I Wonder as I Wander: An Autobiographical Journey*. New York: Rinehart & Co., 1956. 405p.

Reprinted New York: Hill & Wang, 1964.

AU   CSdS   CU   DHU   FTaFA   IU   LU   NN   PPiU   TxU

The poet, dramatist, fiction writer, and essayist portrays his travels and adventures during the 1930s, in places such as California, Cuba, Haiti, Spain, Mexico, China, and Japan. Included is a lengthy section on Hughes' visit to the USSR. [See preceding item.]

122. Hughes, Louis B. (1832-1913). *Thirty Years a Slave: From Bondage to Freedom. The Institution of Slavery as Seen on the Plantation and in the Home of the Planter. Autobiography of Louis Hughes*. Illustrated.

Milwaukee: South Side Printing Co., 1897. 210p.
  Reprinted Detroit: Negro History Press, 1969.
  Reprinted Miami, Fla.: Mnemosyne Publishing Co., 1969.
  Reprinted New York: Negro Universities Press, 1969.
  CU DHU FMU FTaSU NN NjR OClWHi PLuL PPiU WHi
  A male nurse in Milwaukee reveals his slave life in Virginia, Mississippi, Alabama, and Tennessee; his escape to Canada during the Civil War; his employment at various jobs in the Midwest; and his hotel work and laundry business in Milwaukee.

123. Hunter, Jane Edna Harris (1882-1971). *A Nickel and a Prayer*. Introduction by George Bellamy. Cleveland: Elli Kani Publishing Co., 1940. 198p.
  Reprinted Nashville: Parthenon Press, 1940.
  CU MH MiD NN NRU NcD OEac PP OrU ViU
  The founder of the Phillis Wheatley Association in Cleveland and a civil and social service worker there, Hunter precedes a description of her activities with a narrative of her early life in South Carolina, her education at Ferguson and Williams College (South Carolina), and her work as a nurse in South Carolina and Florida.

124. Hurston, Zora Neale (1901-1960). *Dust Tracks on a Road*. Philadelphia: Lippincott, 1942. 294p.
  Reprinted New York: Arno Press, 1969.
  Reprinted Philadelphia: Lippincott, 1971.
  CSt DHU NN NcD OU OrU PPiCl TU WU WvU
  An anthropologist, folklorist, and novelist, Hurston exuberantly depicts her youth in Eatonville, Florida, her education at Howard University and Barnard College, her life in New York City, and her careers. [See Item 352.]

125. Iceberg Slim—see Beck, Robert.

126. Jackson, George Washington (1860?-1940). *A Brief History of the Life and Works of G. W. Jackson; Forty-Five Years Principal of the G. W. Jackson High School, Corsicana, Texas*. Introduction by C. W. Abington. Corsicana, Tex.: The Author, 1938. 44p.
  DHU
  For forty-five years the principal of the high school named after him, Jackson also talks of his slave life in Alabama and his education at Fisk University.

127. Jackson, Henry—see Armstrong, Henry.

128. Jackson, Mahalia (1911-1972), with Evan McLeod Wylie. *Movin' On Up*. Illustrated. Discography. New York: Hawthorn Books, 1966. 219p.
  Revised and reprinted New York: Avon Books, 1969.
  CtHT DHU DLC FTaFA NN PLuL PPi PPiU WHi WU
  The famous gospel singer deals with her youth in New Orleans and Chicago, her work for civil rights organizations, her travels in the U.S.

and Europe, and her career. The 1969 edition updates her life story, and features a revised Discography.

129. Jamal, Hakim Abdullah [formerly Donaldson, Allen] (1931-   ). *From the Dead Level: Malcolm X and Me*. London: Andre Deutsch, 1971. 240p.
    Reprinted New York: Random House, 1972.
    CtH   DLC   PPiCl   PPiU   WvU
    Though Jamal focuses on his contacts with Malcolm X, the Black Muslim leader, he also depicts his early life in Boston, his service with the U.S. Army in New Jersey and Japan, his jobs and experiences in Richmond and Los Angeles, his criminal activities, his term in a Virginia prison, his narcotics addiction, and his work as a linotype operator. His autobiography ends in 1965, with the assassination of Malcolm X.

130. James, Thomas (1804-1891). *Life of Reverend Thomas James, by Himself*. Rochester, N.Y.: Post Express Printing Co., 1886. 23p.
    NN   NIC   NR
    In his very brief autobiography, this African Methodist Episcopal minister in Rochester, New York, highlights his antislavery work. He was born a slave in New York State, but escaped to Canada in 1821. He held ministerial positions in New York State, Massachusetts, and Washington, D.C.; and during the Civil War he worked in Kentucky for the U.S. Government helping freed and refugee slaves.

131. Jamison, Monroe Franklin (b. 1848). *Autobiography and Work of Bishop M. F. Jamison, D.D. ("Uncle Joe"), Editor, Publisher, and Church Extension Secretary: A Narration of His Whole Career from the Cradle to the Bishopric of the Colored M.E. Church in America*. Introduction by George L. Tyus. Illustrated. Nashville: The Author, 1912. 206p.
    DHU   IEG   N   TxU   ViU
    A bishop in the Colored Methodist Episcopal Church narrates his slave life in Georgia and Alabama, his editorship of church publications, and his religious work in Texas.

132. Johnson, James Weldon (1871-1938). *Along This Way: The Autobiography of James Weldon Johnson*. Illustrated. Index. New York: Viking Press, 1933. 418p.
    Reprinted New York: Penguin Books, 1941.
    Reprinted New York: Compass Books–Viking Press, 1968.
    CSdS   DHU   FTaFA   NN   OTU   PLuL   PPiCl   PPiU   WU   WvU
    For fourteen years the secretary of the NAACP, Johnson also distinguished himself as a poet, novelist, essayist, lecturer, song writer, lawyer, diplomat, teacher, and education administrator. He was born and reared in Jacksonville, Florida, educated at Atlanta University and Columbia University, taught and was a school principal in Florida, was

a U.S. consul in Venezuela and Nicaragua, and toward the end of his life filled a professorship at Fisk University.

133. Johnson, Jesse J. (1914-   ). *Ebony Brass: An Autobiography of Negro Frustration Amid Aspiration*. Appendix. New York: William-Frederick Press, 1967. 141p.

　　CSdS   DHU   DLC   FTaFA   PLuL   PPi   PPiU   WHi   WU   WvU

　　A retired U.S. Army lieutenant colonel, born and reared in Mississippi, concentrates on his twenty-year military career and on the conditions of Negroes in the Army.

134. Johnson, [John] Jack [Arthur] (1878-1946). *Jack Johnson, In the Ring and Out*. Introductions by "Tad," Ed. W. Smith, Damon Runyon, and Mrs. Jack Johnson. Illustrated. Chicago: National Sports Publishing Co., 1927. 259p.

　　Reprinted Detroit: Gale Research Co., 1972.

　　Reprinted as *Jack Johnson Is a Dandy: An Autobiography*. New York: Chelsea House Publishers, 1969; and New York: Signet Books— New American Library, 1970.

　　DHU   FTaFA   GU   IU   IaU   MH   MiU   NN   NcD   PLuL

　　The former world champion heavyweight boxer from Texas characterizes his youth, the excitement of his international boxing career, his romances, his exile from the U.S., and his prison experiences.

135. Johnson, Marguerite—see Angelou, Maya.

136. Johnson, Thomas Lewis (b. 1836). *Africa for Christ. Twenty-Eight Years a Slave*. Introduction by Edward Stroud Smith. Illustrated. London: Alexander & Shepheard, 1892. 110p.

　　NN

　　A former Virginia slave narrates his slave life and his work as a Baptist missionary in Denver, Chicago, Africa, and the British Isles. [See next item.]

137. Johnson, Thomas Lewis (b. 1836). *Twenty-Eight Years a Slave; or, the Story of My Life in Three Continents*. Introductions by Sir George Williams and Edward Stroud Smith. Illustrated. Bournemouth, England: W. Mate & Sons, 1909. 266p.

　　CU   InU   NN   NcD

　　Retelling the story of his slave life in Virginia and of his religious work in the U.S., Africa, and the British Isles, Johnson adds events in his private life and missionary vocation in the British Isles. He became a British subject in 1900. [See preceding item.]

138. Jones, Cleon Joseph (1942-   ), with Ed Hershey. *Cleon*. Editor's Note by Ed Hershey. Illustrated. Appendix. New York: Coward-McCann, 1970. 191p.

　　DLC   MB   NjP   PPi   WHi

　　Dealing primarily with his professional baseball career with the New York Mets, Jones also mentions his boyhood near Mobile, Alabama, and his college days at Alabama Agricultural and Mechanical College.

139. Jones, Laurence Clifton (1884-   ). *Up Through Difficulties*. Braxton, Miss.: Pine Torch, 1913. 79p.

    IaHi

    The principal of the Piney Woods (Mississippi) Country Life School portrays his early years in Missouri and Iowa, his education at the Central Iowa Business College and the University of Iowa, his teaching years in Mississippi, and his work at the school which he founded in 1909. [See next item.]

140. Jones, Laurence Clifton (1884-   ). *Piney Woods and Its Story*. Introduction by S. S. McClure. Illustrated. New York: Fleming H. Revell, 1922. 154p.

    CSdS   DHU   GAU   NN   OCl   PLuL   PPiU   TU   WHi   WvU

    After retelling the story of his life in Missouri, Iowa, and Mississippi, Jones devotes the second half to describing his later activities at Piney Woods Country Life School. [See preceding item.]

141. Jones, Thomas Alfred (1904-   ). *The Secret*. New York: Comet Press Books, 1958. 127p.

    DHU   DLC   NN   NNC   WHi

    The author writes of his life of petty crime in Washington, D.C., after accounting for his early years in North Carolina.

142. Jordan, Lewis Garnett (1854?-1939). *On Two Hemispheres: Bits from the Life Story of Lewis G. Jordan, as Told by Himself*. Introduction by Adam Clayton Powell, Sr. Illustrated. N.P.: n.p., n.d. [1935?]. 80p.

    DHU   NN

    A Baptist minister and missionary, Jordan describes his slave life in Mississippi, and his religious work in Mississippi, Louisiana, Texas, Philadelphia, Africa, and Europe.

143. Joseph-Gaudet, Frances—see Gaudet, Frances Joseph.

144. Julian, Hubert Fauntleroy (1897-   ). *Black Eagle*. As told to and Preface by John Bulloch. Illustrated. Index. London: Jarrolds, 1964. 200p.

    DLC   NN   PLuL   WU

    An aviator and international dealer in arms and munitions after World War II, born and reared in Trinidad, Julian also discusses his education in London and Montreal, his experiences in the U.S. as a stunt flyer and parachutist during the 1920s, his adventures as a flyer in Ethiopia and Finland during the 1930s, and his military service in the U.S. Army during World War II.

145. Keckley, Elizabeth Hobbs (1824-1907). *Behind the Scenes: Thirty Years a Slave and Four Years in the White House*. Appendix. New York: G. W. Carleton & Co., 1868. 371p.

    Reprinted New York: Arno Press, 1968.

    CSdS   DHU   FTaFA   NN   OTU   PLuL   PPiCl   PPiU   WHi   WvU

The companion and seamstress to Mary Todd Lincoln devotes the greater part of her book to her four years in the White House, but also alludes to her slave life in Virginia and North Carolina, and her experiences in St. Louis. The Appendix contains letters and notes from Mrs. Lincoln to the author.

146. Keene, Royal D. (1895-   ). *The Light Still Shines.* Illustrated. Tribute by T. H. Lea. New York: Carlton Press, 1961. 40p.

DHU   DLC   FTaFA   OCl

This brief autobiography by a Cleveland physician covers his early years in Virginia; his education at Virginia Union University, Shaw University, Meharry Pharmaceutical College, and Meharry Medical College; his service in the U.S. Army during World War I; his career as a pharmacist in North Carolina, Ohio, Virginia, and West Virginia; his various employments in Chicago and Philadelphia; and his experiences in his medical practices in Virginia, West Virginia, and Ohio.

147. King, Coretta Scott (1927-   ). *My Life with Martin Luther King, Jr.* Illustrated. Index. New York: Holt, Rinehart & Winston, 1969. 372p.
Reprinted New York: Avon Books, 1970.

CtHT   DHU   DLC   NN   PLuL   PPi   PPiCl   PPiU   WU   WvU

Primarily an account of her life after 1953 as the wife of civil rights leader The Reverend Martin Luther King, Jr., this book also mentions Mrs. King's youth in Alabama, her collegiate life at Antioch College, and her training at the New England Conservatory of Music. [See Item 361.]

148. Kitt, Eartha Mae (1928-   ). *Thursday's Child.* New York: Duell, Sloan & Pearce, 1956. 250p.

CU   CtY   DHU   FTaFA   IU   MiU   NN   PLuL   PPiU   TxU

The popular singer, dancer, and actress recalls her careers in the U.S. and Europe, after describing her childhood in South Carolina and New York City.

149. Lacy, Leslie Alexander (1937-   ). *The Rise and Fall of a Proper Negro: An Autobiography.* New York: Macmillan, 1970. 244p.
Reprinted New York: Pocket Books, 1971.

DHU   IU   InU   MB   PPiCl   PPiU   ViU   WHi   WU   WvU

While depicting his childhood in a prosperous Louisiana family, his education at a New England college, and his experiences from 1963 to 1966 as an expatriate in West Africa, mostly in Ghana, this college professor and essayist also offers his analysis of racial and political problems in the U.S. and Africa.

150. Lane, Isaac (1834-1937). *Autobiography of Bishop Isaac Lane, LL.D.; with a Short History of the C.M.E. Church in America and of Methodism.* Introduction by J. Arthur Hamlett. Illustrated. Nashville: M.E. Church, South, 1916. 192p.

DLC   IEG   ViU   WHi

A bishop in the Colored Methodist Episcopal Church from 1873 to 1914 and one of its early organizers, Lane outlines his slave life in Tennessee, his efforts to found and build Lane College in Tennessee, and his religious work in Tennessee, Louisiana, Oklahoma, and Texas. His autobiography also contains sketches of the lives of other bishops in the Colored Methodist Episcopal Church.

151. Langston, John Mercer (1829-1897). *From the Virginia Plantation to the National Capitol; or, the First and Only Negro Representative in Congress from the Old Dominion*. Illustrated. Hartford, Conn.: American Publishing Co., 1894. 534p.

Reprinted New York: Arno Press, 1969.
Reprinted New York: Bergman Publishers, 1969.
Reprinted New York: Kraus Reprint Co., 1969.
CSdS   CtY   DHU   IaU   NN   NjP   OU   OrU   PLuL   PPiU
In his third-person autobiography, the first Negro elected from Virginia to the U.S. House of Representatives recalls his political career, his youth in Virginia, his schooling in Cincinnati and education at Oberlin College, his work as a lawyer in Ohio, his duties as minister to Haiti, his teaching experiences at Howard University, and his administrative achievements as president of the Virginia Normal and Collegiate Institute.

151a. Latta, Morgan London (b. 1853). *The History of My Life and Work: Autobiography*. Introduction by George Daniel. Illustrated. Raleigh, N.C.: The Author, 1903. 371p.

Revised and reprinted Raleigh, N.C.: The Author, 1924.
DLC   NcRR   WvU
An ex-slave in North Carolina who later attended Shaw University and then was for many years a schoolteacher writes primarily on his work as head of Latta University in West Raleigh, North Carolina, an institution he founded in 1892. He also tells of his experiences in the Raleigh area and alludes to his visit to England and France. The revised edition of his autobiography mentions events in his life after 1903 and publishes long essays by Carter G. Woodson and Frederick E. Drinker. Latta was also a minister.

152. Lee, Reba [pseud.] (1930-   ). *I Passed for White*. As told to and Foreword by Mary Hastings Bradley. New York: Longmans, Green, 1955. 274p.

CU   DHU   NN   NcD   PLuL   PP   PPi   PPiU   TxU   ViU
Passing as a white person for most of her life, the author portrays the pains and joys of her years in Chicago and New York City.

153. Lewis, Henry Harrison (b. 1840). *Life of Rev. H. H. Lewis; Giving a History of His Early Life and Services in the Ministry. Written and Compiled by Himself*. Philadelphia: S. L. Nichols, 1877. 54p.

DHU   NN

Born free in Maryland and later to become a minister in the African Methodist Episcopal Church, Lewis outlines his youth in Maryland and Delaware, as well as his religious work in Delaware and the Philadelphia area.

154. Lewis, Joseph Vance. *Out of the Ditch: A True Story of an Ex-Slave.* Illustrated. Houston: Rein & Sons Co., Printer, 1910. 154p.

   NN   TxH

   A Houston lawyer and self-styled physician portrays his slave life in Louisiana, his college days at Leland University, his training in the law at the University of Michigan, the Chicago School of Law, and the London (England) Lane School of Law, his political activities in Chicago for the Republican Party, his travels in Europe, and his professional work in New Orleans and Texas.

155. Little, Malcolm—see Malcolm X.

156. Louis, [Joseph] Joe [formerly Barrow, Joseph Louis] (1914-). *My Life Story*. Editorial assistance by Chester L. Washington and Haskell Cohen. Illustrated. New York: Duell, Sloan & Pearce, 1947. 188p.

   Reprinted as *The Joe Louis Story*. New York: Grosset & Dunlap, 1955.

   CtH   DHU   DLC   FTaFA   NN   NcSalL   PLuL   PPi   WHi

   Concentrating on his boxing career, the world heavyweight champion also depicts his youth in Alabama and Detroit and his military life in the U.S. Army during World War II.

157. Love, Nat (1854-1921). *The Life and Adventures of Nat Love, Better Known in the Cattle Country as "Deadwood Dick," by Himself: A True History of Slavery Days, Life on the Great Cattle Ranges and on the Plains of the "Wild and Woolly" West, Based on Facts, and Personal Experiences of the Author*. Illustrated. Los Angeles: The Author, 1907. 162p.

   Reprinted New York: Arno Press, 1968.

   CSdS   DHU   DLC   OTU   PLuL   PPi   PPiU   WHi   WvU

   Perhaps somewhat exaggerated, this account of the adventures of a railroad car worker covers his slave life in Tennessee and his experiences as a cowboy from 1869 to 1890.

158. Lynch, John Roy (1847-1939). *Reminiscences of an Active Life: The Autobiography of John Roy Lynch*. Edited and Introduction by John Hope Franklin. Notes. Index. Chicago: Univ. of Chicago Press, 1970. 521p.

   DLC   ICU   PPiCl   PPiU   WHi   WvU

   A Chicago lawyer and realtor and the first Negro elected into the U.S. House of Representatives from Mississippi, Lynch writes of his slave life in Louisiana and Mississippi, his political activities for the Republican Party in Mississippi, his experiences in the Mississippi legislature, his duties as a U.S. Army officer during and after the Spanish-

American War, and his business and legal activities in Mississippi and Chicago. [See Item 365.]

159. Lynk, Miles Vandahurst (1871-1957?). *Sixty Years of Medicine; or, the Life and Times of Dr. Miles V. Lynk: An Autobiography*. Introduction by E. H. Jones. Illustrated. Index. Memphis: Twentieth Century Press, 1951. 125p.

　　DHU DLC NN

　　A physician and teacher focuses upon his achievements at the University of West Tennessee, a medical school he founded. He also describes his early life in Tennessee and his education at Meharry Medical College.

160. McDonald, [Emanuel] Sam [B.] (1884-1957). *Sam McDonald's Farm: Stanford Reminiscences*. Preface by Tully C. Knoles. Illustrated. Index. Stanford, Cal.: Stanford Univ. Press, 1954. 422p.

　　CSt DHU IU NN OOxM

　　Associated with Stanford University from 1903 in various service capacities, McDonald reminisces about his work and experiences there and refers to his youth in Louisiana and Southern California and his life as a California farmer and steamship laborer.

161. McKay, Claude (1890-1948). *A Long Way from Home: An Autobiography*. New York: Lee Furman, 1937. 354p.

　　Reprinted New York: Arno Press, 1969.

　　Reprinted New York: Harvest Books—Harcourt, Brace & World, 1970.

　　CtH DHU NN PLuL PPi PPiCl PPiU ViHaI WU WvU

　　The famous Jamaica-born poet and fiction writer concentrates on his life during the 1920s and 1930s, when he was active in the Harlem Renaissance and traveled in Africa, Europe, and the USSR.

162. Magee, J[ames] H. (b. 1839). *The Night of Affliction and Morning of Recovery: An Autobiography*. Cincinnati: The Author, 1873. 173p.

　　Reprinted Miami, Fla.: Mnemosyne Publishing Co., 1969.

　　DHU DLC NN PLuL PPi WHi

　　Offering a lengthy account of his travels in England after the Civil War, a Baptist minister also describes his early life in Illinois, and his religious work in Toronto, Illinois, Nashville, and Cincinnati.

163. Malcolm X [formerly Little, Malcolm] (1925-1965), with the assistance of and Epilogue by Alex Haley. *The Autobiography of Malcolm X*. Introduction by M. S. Handler. New York: Grove Press, 1965. 455p.

　　Reprinted New York: Evergreen Black Cat Books—Grove Press, 1966.

　　CSdS DHU FTaFA NN OTU PLuL PPi PPiU WHi WU

　　This influential autobiography of the famous religious and racial leader, assassinated in 1965, tells of his activities as a Black Muslim minister, his youth in Omaha and Michigan, his varied jobs and his criminal life in Boston and New York City, and his intellectual and spiritual awakening during a seven-year imprisonment. [See Item 366.]

164. Mallory, William (1826-1905?). *Old Plantation Days*. Illustrated. N.P. [Hamilton, Ont.?] : n.p., n.d. [1902?]. 56p.

DLC   NcU

A former slave in North Carolina and Louisiana, Mallory narrates his escape to Canada in 1860, his service as a Union Army officer during the Civil War, his business and political affairs in Canada, and his religious missionary work in Africa. This pamphlet contains poems by the author.

165. Maloney, Arnold Hamilton (1888-1955). *Amber Gold: An Adventure in Autobiography*. Introductions by T. M. Kelshall, J. A. Scrimgeour, Lionel F. Artis, and Tom Phillips. Index. Boston: Meador Publishing Co., 1946. 448p.

DHU   DLC   NN   PLuL   PU   WHi

A professor at Howard University from 1931, head of the Department of Pharmacology, an Episcopal minister, and an essayist depicts his early life in Trinidad; his education at Naparima College (Trinidad), Lincoln University (Pennsylvania), the General Theological Seminary (Philadelphia), Indiana University, the University of Wisconsin, Syracuse University, and the University of Buffalo; his ministerial duties in Maryland, Indiana, and New York State; and his teaching tenure at Wilberforce University and Howard University. Some chapters of his autobiography consist of his essays on a variety of topics, such as philosophy and literature.

166. Malvin, John (1795-1880). *Autobiography of John Malvin: A Narrative, Containing an Authentic Account of His Fifty Years' Struggle in the State of Ohio in Behalf of the American Slave, and the Equal Rights of All Men Before the Law Without Reference to Race or Color; Forty-Seven Years of Said Time Being Expended in the City of Cleveland*. Cleveland: Leader Printing Co., 1879. 42p.

Reprinted as *North Into Freedom: The Autobiography of John Malvin, Free Negro, 1795-1880*. Edited, Introduction, and Notes by Allan Peskin. Cleveland: Western Reserve University Press, 1966.

CSdS   DLC   FTaSU   NN   NcSalL   OTU   PLuL   PPi   WHi   WU

Born and reared a freeman in Virginia, Malvin later moved to Ohio, where he became an abolitionist, civil rights leader, and political reformist in Cleveland.

167. Marrs, Elijah Preston (1840-1910). *Life and History of the Rev. Elijah P. Marrs*. Louisville: Bradley & Gilbert Co., 1885. 147p.

Reprinted Miami, Fla.: Mnemosyne Publishing Co., 1969.

DHU   DLC   InU   PPiU   TNF

A Kentucky teacher, educational administrator, and Baptist minister

describes his careers, his slave life in Kentucky, and his combat experiences in the Union Army during the Civil War.

168. Mason, Isaac (b. 1822). *Life of Isaac Mason as a Slave*. Worcester,
Mass.: The Author, 1893. 74p.

    Reprinted Miami, Fla.: Mnemosyne Publishing Co., 1969.

    DHU DLC ICU NN PLuL PPiU WHi

    A resident of Worcester, Massachusetts, portrays his slave life in
Maryland and his later adventures in Canada, Haiti, Philadelphia, and
Worcester.

169. Mays, Benjamin Elijah (1895-   ). *Born to Rebel: An Autobiography*.
Introduction by Samuel DuBois Cook. Illustrated. Appendixes. New
York: Scribner's, 1971. 380p.

    Reprinted New York: Scribner's, 1972.

    IU IaU KyU MoSW NRU NcU PPiU ViU WU Wa

    In analyzing the history of racial problems in the U.S., this religious
and education leader also covers his early years in South Carolina, his
studies at Virginia Union University, Bates College, and the University
of Chicago, his teaching career at State College (South Carolina),
Howard University, and Morehouse College (where he later served as
president), his work for the Tampa, Florida, Urban League, his administrative duties for the YMCA, and his religious vocation as a Baptist
minister.

170. Mays, [William] Willie [Howard] (1931-   ). *Born to Play Ball*. As told
to and Introduction by Charles Einstein. Illustrated. New York: Putnam's, 1955. 168p.

    CtH FTaFA NN NcD NcSalL OCl OOxM PP PPi ViU

    The famous professional baseball player, born and reared in Alabama,
focuses on his career with the New York Giants. [See next item.]

171. Mays, [William] Willie [Howard] (1931-   ). *Willie Mays: My Life In
and Out of Baseball*. As told to Charles Einstein. Illustrated. Appendix.
New York: Dutton, 1966. 320p.

    Revised and reprinted Greenwich, Conn.: Crest Books—Fawcett,
1973.

    CSdS CtH DHU DLC FTaFA NN PPi WHi

    Mays retells his earlier story, then continues the account of his base-
ball career with the New York Giants and the San Francisco Giants.
The revised edition adds brief chapters covering his career from 1966
to mid-1972, with the San Francisco Giants and the New York Mets.
[See preceding item.]

172. Meredith, James Howard (1933-   ). *Three Years in Mississippi*. Bloomington: Indiana Univ. Press, 1966. 328p.

    CSdS DHU FTaFA InU NN PLuL PPi PPiU WU WvU

    Resourcefully using letters, court transcripts, and mass-media reports,

Meredith documents his successful struggle to matriculate into and later graduate from the University of Mississippi. His story treats primarily the years 1960 through 1963 but also mentions his early life in Mississippi, his service duty in the U.S. Air Force, and his student days at Jackson State College.

173. Micheaux, Oscar (1884-   ). *The Conquest: The Story of a Negro Pioneer*. Illustrated. Lincoln, Neb.: Woodruff Press, 1913. 311p.
    Reprinted College Park, Md.: McGrath Publishing Co., 1969.
    Reprinted Miami, Fla.: Mnemosyne Publishing Co., 1969.
    CSt   NN   NcU   PPiCl   PPiU   WU
    Later to become a novelist, publisher, and film director, Micheaux takes the pseudonym "Devereaux" to describe his early years in Illinois and his experiences as a homesteader, farmer, and businessman in South Dakota.

174. Miles, Floyd Alexander, Jr. (1928-   ). *Black Tracks: Nineteen Years on the Mainline*. As told to Irene Burk Harrell. Plainfield, N.J.: Logos International, 1972. 115p.
    DLC
    The author speaks of his childhood, adolescence, petty criminal activities, and the long period of his drug addiction in Harlem. He also served terms in prisons. Praising the impact of his religious conversion on his successful effort to cure his drug addiction, he then describes his community service work in New York City and Plainfield, New Jersey.

175. Mingus, Charles (1922-   ). *Beneath the Underdog: His World as Composed by Mingus*. Edited by Nel King. New York: Knopf, 1971. 366p.
    Reprinted New York: Bantam Books, 1972.
    DLC   MB   MH   MeB   MiEM   NjP   PPiU   WvU
    The jazz musician and composer deals with both his private and professional life, including his youth in Los Angeles and his criminal activities.

176. Mix, Mrs. Edward [Sarah A.] (1832-1884). *In Memory of Departed Worth: The Life of Mrs. Edward Mix, Written by Herself in 1880*. Appendix. Torrington, Conn.: Press of Register Printing Co., 1884. 24p.
    DHU
    In celebrating her religious faith and describing her mystical experiences, the author recalls incidents in a life she spent in New York State and Connecticut.

177. Moody, Anne (1940-   ). *Coming of Age in Mississippi*. New York: Dial Press, 1968. 348p.
    Reprinted New York: Dell, 1970.
    DHU   ICU   IaU   MU   NIC   NcRR   PLuL   PPiCl   PPiU   WU
    A worker for the NAACP and the Congress of Racial Equality

remembers her civil rights activities in Louisiana and Mississippi, her childhood in Mississippi, and her education at Natchez College and Tougaloo College.

178. Moore, Archie Lee (1916-   ). *The Archie Moore Story*. Illustrated. Appendix. New York: McGraw-Hill, 1960. 240p.

CtH   DHU   FTaFA   ICU   MiU   NN   NNC   NcRR   PP   PPi

The former light-heavyweight boxing champion of the world focuses on his career, after telling of his boyhood in Mississippi and St. Louis, his criminal activities, and his experiences in the Missouri State Reform School. [See next item.]

179. Moore, Archie Lee (1916-   ), and Leonard B. Pearl. *Any Boy Can: The Archie Moore Story*. Foreword and Afterword by Leonard B. Pearl. Illustrated. Appendix. Englewood Cliffs, N.J.: Prentice-Hall, 1971. 263p.

CtH   DLC   PPi   WU

Moore retells the story of his youth and boxing career, adding accounts of his work for the Boy Scouts of America and his achievements as founder of and counselor for Any Boy Can, a club in California whose goal is to motivate youngsters to lead productive and moral lives. [See preceding item.]

180. Moore, Martha Edith Bannister (1910-   ). *Unmasked: The Story of My Life on Both Sides of the Race Barrier*. New York: Exposition Press, 1964. 106p.

DHU   DLC   FTaFA   NN   PPiU   WHi

A Pittsburgh woman who often passed for white presents a somewhat disjointed account of her various employments, her job in the U.S. Civil Service, her efforts for the Republican Party, and her activities for the Urban League and the NAACP.

181. Morant, John James (1870-1961). *Mississippi Minister*. Illustrated. New York: Vantage Press, 1958. 80p.

DHU   GEU   MsU   NN   NNC   NcD   NcRR   PU   TxDaM   WHi

An African Methodist Episcopal minister, born in Alabama, describes his church work in Mississippi and his administrative duties as dean of the E. W. Lampton Theological Seminary's School of Religion (Vicksburg, Mississippi) and as dean of the School of Religion at Campbell College (Jackson, Mississippi).

182. Morgan, Gordon Daniel (1931-   ). *Poverty Without Bitterness*. Jefferson City, Mo.: New Scholars Press, 1969. 63p.

ArU   DHU

A sociologist at the University of Arkansas recalls his boyhood in Arkansas, his education at the Arkansas Agricultural, Mechanical and Normal College and at the University of Minnesota, his military service with the U.S. Army in Korea, and his years as a teacher and administrator in Arkansas public schools and later as a college professor. [See Item 368.]

183. Morrow, E[verett] Frederic (1909-   ). *Way Down South Up North.* Philadelphia: Pilgrim Press—United Church Press, 1973. 128p.

 DLC   PPiCl   PPiU

 A business executive who once served as an administrator in the WhiteHouse under President Dwight D. Eisenhower here remembers his childhood and adolescence in Hackensack, New Jersey. [See Item 369.]

184. Morton, Lena Beatrice (1901-   ). *My First Sixty Years: Passion for Wisdom.* New York: Philosophical Library, 1965. 175p.

 DHU   DLC   FTaFA   NN   NNC   PPi   PPiU   TxU   WU

 Born and reared in Kentucky and educated at the University of Cincinnati and Western Reserve University, the author depicts her childhood and her career in Cincinnati before assuming teaching positions at various Southern colleges. Her autobiography includes her essays on education and on racial topics, some of her speeches, and a selection of her poems.

185. Moton, Robert Russa (1867-1940). *Finding a Way Out: An Autobiography.* Index. Garden City, N.Y.: Doubleday, Page, 1920. 296p.

 Reprinted College Park, Md.: McGrath Publishing Co., 1969.

 Reprinted New York: Negro Universities Press, 1969.

 DHU   MH   MU   PLuL   PPi   PPiU   ViHaI   ViU   WHi   WvU

 The autobiography of this distinguished scholar, educator, college administrator, and lawyer accounts for his early life in Virginia, his education at Hampton Institute, his teaching and administrative work there, and his responsibilities as the successor to Booker T. Washington as principal of Tuskegee Institute.

186. Mulzac, Hugh N. (1886-1971). *A Star to Steer By.* As told to Louis Burnham and Norval Welch. Illustrated. New York: International Publishers, 1963. 251p.

 CtH   DHU   DLC   NN   WHi

 The first Negro to earn his first mate's license, in 1918, and the first Negro to captain a ship in the U.S. Merchant Marine, in 1942, Mulzac was born in the British West Indies. His autobiography features accounts of his sea adventures, his combat experiences during World War II, his political activities in New York City for the American Labor Party, and his efforts to earn a living in Harlem after his retirement from the sea.

187. Newton, Alexander Herritage (b. 1837). *Out of the Briars: An Autobiography and Sketch of the Twenty-Ninth Regiment, Connecticut Volunteers.* Introduction by J. P. Sampson. Illustrated. Philadelphia: A.M.E. Book Concern, 1910. 269p.

 Reprinted Miami, Fla.: Mnemosyne Publishing Co., 1969.

DHU   DLC   NN   PPiU

An African Methodist Episcopal minister describes his early years as a freeman in North Carolina, his jobs and abolitionist activities in New York City and Connecticut, his combat service in the Union Army during the Civil War, and his religious work in New England, the South, and, in particular, New Jersey. The last third of his autobiography contains some of his essays, sermons, and church resolutions.

188. Newton, Huey Pierce (1942-   ), with the assistance of J. Herman Blake. *Revolutionary Suicide*. Illustrated. New York: Harcourt Brace Jovanovich, 1973. 333p.

   DLC   PPiCl

   The cofounder of the Black Panther Party for Self-Defense in 1966, Newton begins by treating his youth in Louisiana and Oakland, California. He later attended Oakland City College, but was also a petty criminal who spent time in jail. Much of his autobiography deals with his party activities in California, his imprisonment for allegedly killing a police officer, and the trials and legal appeals which led to the dismissal of charges against him in 1970. Also included is a brief account of his visit to the People's Republic of China in 1971.

189. Owens, [Jones] Jesse [Cleveland] (1913-   ), with Paul G. Neimark. *Blackthink: My Life as Black Man and White Man*. New York: William Morrow, 1970. 215p.

   Reprinted New York: Pocket Books, 1971.

   CSt   DHU   IaU   InU   KU   KyU   MH   NjP   PPiU   ViU

   While commenting on a variety of racial topics, the track star of the 1936 Olympics also alludes to his youth in Alabama and Cleveland, his college years at Ohio State University, his athletic career, and his business ventures. [See next item and Item 373.]

190. Owens, [Jones] Jesse [Cleveland] (1913-   ), with Paul G. Neimark. *The Jesse Owens Story*. Index. New York: Putnam's, 1970. 109p.

   CtH   DLC   PPi   WvU

   In a brief volume prepared primarily for young readers, the ex-Olympic track star recounts the major events of his life. [See preceding item and Item 373.]

191. Paige, LeRoy "Satchel" Robert (1906-   ). *Maybe I'll Pitch Forever*. As told to David Lipman. Illustrated. Garden City, N.Y.: Doubleday, 1962. 285p.

   Reprinted New York: Evergreen Black Cat Books—Grove Press, 1963.
   Reprinted New York: Zebra Books—Grove Press, 1971.

   DHU   DLC   FTaFA   NN   PLuL   PPi

   The famous professional baseball pitcher concentrates on his career with Negro teams and then with the Cleveland Indians, after mentioning his early years in Mobile, Alabama.

192. Parker, Allen (b. 1837?). *Recollections of Slavery Times*. Worcester,

Mass.: Charles W. Burbank & Co., 1895. 96p.

DHU

A laborer in Worcester, Massachusetts, narrates his slave experiences in North Carolina, his escape to the North in 1862, his service in the U.S. Navy, his shipboard jobs, and his life in New Haven, Connecticut, and Worcester.

193. Parks, Gordon Roger (1912-   ). *A Choice of Weapons*. New York: Harper & Row, 1966. 274p.

Reprinted New York: Medallion Books—Berkley Publishing Corp., 1967.

Reprinted New York: Falcon Books—Noble & Noble, 1968.

CtH DHU DLC FTaFA NN PLuL PPi PPiCl PPiU WU

Later a noted photographer, film director, and novelist, Parks here reveals his life through 1943. He was born in rural Kansas and reared there and in St. Paul, Minnesota. Until his work as a professional photographer in Chicago and then for the U.S. Government during World War II, he had been employed in the Midwest and New York City as a piano player, laborer, railroad car waiter, and professional basketball player. [See Items 374 and 375.]

194. Patterson, Floyd (1935-   ), with Milton Gross. *Victory Over Myself*. Illustrated. New York: Bernard Geis Associates, 1962. 244p.

CtH DHU DLC FTaFA NN PLuL PPi PPiU WvU

The former world heavyweight boxing champion focuses on his career, while also mentioning his boyhood in North Carolina and Brooklyn and his detention in a reform school.

195. Patterson, Haywood (1913?-1952), and Earl Conrad. *Scottsboro Boy*. Foreword by Earl Conrad. Illustrated. Appendixes. Garden City, N.Y.: Doubleday, 1950. 309p.

Reprinted New York: Collier Books, 1969.

DHU DLC NN PLuL PPiCl PPiU WHi WvU

One of eight Negro youths accused of raping two white girls in Alabama in 1931, Patterson describes the circumstances surrounding the allegation, the four controversial trials, his life in Alabama prisons, and his escape to a Northern city in 1948.

196. Patterson, Kathryn (1936-   ). *No Time for Tears*. Illustrated. Appendix. Chicago: Johnson Publishing Co., 1965. 109p.

DHU DLC FTaFA NN PPi

Part I of the author's book covers her youth in Centralia, Illinois (where she developed epilepsy), her life in Chicago, and her marriage. Part II portrays her life in Illinois with a hydrocephalic son.

197. Patterson, William L. (1891-   ). *The Man Who Cried Genocide: An Autobiography*. Illustrated. New York: International Publishers, 1971. 223p.

CSt CoU IaU InU KyU MoSW NRU NjR PPiCl WU

Born in San Francisco and reared in Oakland, Patterson received his law degree from the University of California, then practiced in Harlem. He joined the Communist Party and became involved nationally in a variety of quasi-political legal affairs and in civil rights work, founding the Civil Rights Congress. He also initiated the petition to the United Nations charging the U.S. Government with sponsoring genocide against black people.

198. Payne, Daniel Alexander (1811-1893). *Recollections of Seventy Years.* Compiled and arranged by Sarah C. Bierce Scarborough. Edited by C. S. Smith. Introduction by Francis J. Grimké. Illustrated. Nashville: Publishing House of the A.M.E. Sunday School Union, 1888. 335p.
Reprinted New York: Arno Press, 1968.
CSdS DHU DLC NN OTU PLuL PPiCl PPiU WHi WvU
A bishop in the African Methodist Episcopal Church, and the first president of Wilberforce University, Payne describes his distinguished church and academic administrative careers in the East, Midwest, Southwest, and Canada, after discussing his youth as a freeman in South Carolina, his studies at the Lutheran Theological Seminary (Gettysburg, Pennsylvania), his work as a teacher in Philadelphia, and his early ministerial duties in Baltimore and Washington, D.C.

199. Perry, John Edward (1870-1962). *Forty Cords of Wood: Memoirs of a Medical Doctor.* Introduction by John A. Kenney. Illustrated. Jefferson City, Mo.: Lincoln Univ. Press, 1947. 459p.
DHU DLC NN PLuL
A physician in Kansas City, Missouri, treats his early life in Texas, his duties as a teacher in Arkansas, his education at Bishop College and the Post Graduate Medical College (Chicago), and his career in medicine in Missouri. Also described are his civic activities and his responsibilities as a curator of Lincoln University, Missouri.

200. Peyton, Thomas Roy (1897-1969). *Quest for Dignity: An Autobiography of a Negro Doctor.* Los Angeles: Warren F. Lewis, 1950. 156p.
Reprinted Los Angeles: Publishers Western, 1963.
CSdS DHU DLC NN PPiU WHi
Born and reared in Brooklyn, a graduate of the Long Island College of Medicine, Peyton interrupted his early medical practices in New York City and Canada to perform as a singer, piano player, and band leader in Europe. He later resumed his practice in Philadelphia, then in Los Angeles, finally in Brazil. His autobiography ends as he returns to the U.S. to reestablish himself as a doctor in Los Angeles.

201. Phillips, Charles Henry (1858-1951). *From the Farm to the Bishopric: An Autobiography.* Nashville: Parthenon Press, 1932. 308p.
DLC NN OCl ViHal
A bishop in the Colored Methodist Episcopal Church writes of his early life in Georgia; his education at Atlanta University, Central

Tennessee College, Walden University, and Meharry College (where he was trained in both religion and medicine), his experiences as a teacher in Tennessee, and his church work in Memphis, Louisville, the South, Midwest, Southwest, and Far West.

202. Pickens, William (1881-1954). *The Heir of Slaves: An Autobiography*. Boston: Pilgrim Press, 1911. 138p.

    DHU   DLC   FTaFA   NN   ViHaI

    Pickens' memoir covers his youth in South Carolina and Arkansas, his education at Talladega College and Yale University, and his teaching experiences at Talladega College. [See next item.]

203. Pickens, William (1881-1954). *Bursting Bonds*. Boston: Jordan & More Press, 1923. 222p.

    DLC   FTaFA   NN   PLuL   PPi   PPiU   WHi   WvU

    Pickens continues his story, as a professor at Talladega College and then Wiley University, an administrator at Morgan College (Baltimore), and a leader in the activities of the NAACP. [See preceding item.]

204. Pope, Oliver R. (1876-   ). *Chalk Dust*. New York: Pageant Press, 1967. 219p.

    CSdS   CtY   DLC   NcSalL   PLuL

    Treating the years from 1912 to 1947, Pope writes of his successes, failures, and problems as a teacher in and then a supervising principal of Negro schools in a Southern town he calls "Duraton" (probably Rocky Mount, North Carolina).

205. Powell, Adam Clayton, Sr. (1865-1953). *Against the Tide: An Autobiography*. Introduction by William P. Hayes. New York: Richard R. Smith, 1938. 327p.

    DHU   DLC   FTaFA   NN   PLuL   ViHaI   WHi   WvU

    Retired from the pastorship of the Abyssinian Baptist Church in Harlem, the author describes his early years in Virginia, West Virginia, and Ohio; his education at Howard University and Virginia Union University; and his ministerial life in Philadelphia, New York City, and New Haven, Connecticut. He also provides an extensive account of his trip in 1924 to Europe and the Middle East. [See next item.]

206. Powell, Adam Clayton, Jr. (1908-1972). *Adam by Adam: The Autobiography of Adam Clayton Powell, Jr.* Illustrated. Index. New York: Dial Press, 1971. 260p.

    CtH   DLC   PPi   PPiU   WHi   WU   WvU

    Born in New Haven, Connecticut, but reared in New York City, Powell was educated at Colgate University and Columbia University. He became a Baptist minister in Harlem, later assuming his retired father's position, and then engaged in politics as a Democrat. He was elected first to the New York City Council before his lengthy and often controversial tenure in the U.S. House of Representatives beginning in 1944. [See preceding item.]

207. Powell, William Jenifer (1899-1942). *Black Wings*. Foreword by Floyd
C. Covington. Illustrated. Appendix. Los Angeles: Ivan Deach, Jr.,
1934. 218p.

   DHU   DLC   NN   NcD   NcGA

   Using the name "Bill Brown" in his third-person autobiography, the
author concentrates on his adventures as a flyer in California, after his
education at the University of Illinois and the Warren College of Aero-
nautics (Los Angeles). He helped to found the Bessie Coleman Aero
Clubs of Los Angeles, and he wrote and produced a play about
Negroes in aviation. His book focuses primarily on the period 1927 to
1933.

208. Proctor, Henry Hugh (1868-1933). *Between Black and White: Autobiographical Sketches*. Introduction by S. Parkes Cadman. Illustrated.
Boston: Pilgrim Press, 1925. 189p.

   Reprinted Freeport, N.Y.: Books for Libraries Press, 1972.

   DHU   DLC   NN   PPiU   ViHal   WHi

   Frequently discussing racial issues in his autobiography, this Congre-
gational minister also depicts his youth in Tennessee, his education at
Fisk University and the Yale University Divinity School, and his religious work in Atlanta and Brooklyn.

209. Randolph, Peter (1825?-1897). *From Slave Cabin to the Pulpit: The
Autobiography of Rev. Peter Randolph: The Southern Question Illustrated and Sketches of Slave Life*. Boston: James H. Earle, 1893. 200p.

   DLC   NN   PLuL   ViHal   WvU

   Born into slavery in Virginia, Randolph was freed in 1847 and moved
to Boston. His memoirs extensively treat his life as a slave and also
cover his Baptist ministerial work in Massachusetts, Connecticut, New
York State, Rhode Island, and Richmond, Virginia, his study of the
law, and his duties as a justice of the peace in Boston. [See Item 451.]

210. Ransom, Reverdy Cassius (1861-1959). *The Pilgrimage of Harriet
Ransom's Son*. Index. Nashville: Sunday School Union, 1949. 336p.

   DHU   DLC   NN   ViU   WHi

   Born and reared in Ohio, educated at Wilberforce University and
Oberlin College, Ransom was later ordained a minister in the African
Methodist Episcopal Church and elected a bishop in 1924. He was also
a civil rights leader, especially for the NAACP. His autobiography features extensive coverage of his religious work in such areas as Western
Pennsylvania, Cleveland, Chicago, Boston, New York City, Nashville,
and Wilberforce, Ohio. He was active in Republican Party affairs and
was appointed a commissioner on the Ohio Board of Pardon and
Parole. [See Item 382.]

211. Ray, Emma J. Smith (1859-1930). *Twice Sold, Twice Ransomed:
Autobiography of Mr. and Mrs. L. P. Ray*. Introduction by C. E.
McReynolds. Illustrated. Chicago: Free Methodist Publishing House,

1926. 320p.

Reprinted Freeport, N.Y.: Books for Libraries Press, 1971.

DLC   NN   PP   PPiU

A religious evangelist, revival leader, faith healer, missionary, and activist in the Woman's Christian Temperance Union describes her slave life in Missouri, her years in Kansas, and her community and religious work, especially in Seattle after 1889. She was affiliated with the African Methodist Episcopal Church and the Free Methodist Church.

212. Reeves, Donald (1952-   ). *Notes of a Processed Brother*. Appendix. New York: Pantheon Books, 1971. 480p.

Reprinted New York: Discus Books—Avon Books, 1973.

CtH   DLC   PPi   PPiCl   PPiU   WU   WvU

An undergraduate student at Cornell University briefly portrays his childhood in Detroit and his schooling in Jamaica and New York City, before devoting the major part of his narrative to the 1969-1970 academic year, during which he led the movement to establish a bill of rights for students in the New York City public high schools. He sensitively reveals his burgeoning intellectual life and racial consciousness.

213. Robeson, Paul (1898-   ). *Here I Stand*. Appendix. New York: Othello Associates, 1958. 128p.

Reprinted Boston: Beacon Press, 1971.

CU   CtY   DHU   MH   NN   NcD   NcSalL   PLuL   PPiCl   WHi

Interspersed in the autobiography of this noted concert singer and actor are essays and comments on controversial racial and political issues. His career led him throughout the world, after his boyhood in New Jersey and his education at Rutgers University. He lived in London from 1927 to 1939. [See Item 387.]

214. Robinson, Frank (1935-   ), with Al Silverman. *My Life Is Baseball*. Illustrated. Garden City, N.Y.: Doubleday, 1968. 225p.

DLC   PPi

A professional baseball player focuses on his career with the Cincinnati Reds and the Baltimore Orioles, after touching on his youth in Oakland, California.

215. Robinson, James Herman (1907-   ). *Road Without Turning: An Autobiography*. New York: Farrar, Straus, 1950. 312p.

DHU   DLC   NN   PLuL   PPiU   WHi   WvU

A Presbyterian clergyman describes his ministerial, civil rights, and community activities in New York City, after portraying his early years in Tennessee and Ohio, and his education at Lincoln University (Pennsylvania).

216. Robinson, [John] Jackie [Roosevelt] (1919-1972). *Jackie Robinson: My Own Story*. As told to Wendell Smith. Foreword by Branch Rickey. Illustrated. New York: Greenberg Publisher, 1948. 172p.

DHU   DLC   FTaFA   NN   NcSalL   PLuL   PPi

The first Negro to play baseball in a white professional league writes of his athletic career in Kansas City and Montreal and as a member of the Brooklyn Dodgers. His story primarily covers the years 1945 through 1947. [See next two items.]

217. Robinson, [John] Jackie [Roosevelt] (1919-1972), and Alfred Duckett. *Breakthrough to the Big League: The Story of Jackie Robinson.* Illustrated. Index. New York: Harper & Row, 1965. 178p.

CSdS   DLC   FTaFA   NN   PPi

In this book for young readers, Robinson describes not only his career in professional baseball but also his youth in Georgia and California, his college years at the University of California at Los Angeles, and his military service in the U.S. Army during World War II. [See preceding item and next item.]

218. Robinson, [John] Jackie [Roosevelt] (1919-1972). *I Never Had It Made.* As told to Alfred Duckett. New York: Putnam's, 1972. 287p.

CtH   DLC   PPiU

The ex-professional baseball player retells the story of his youth and his career, adding an account of his responsibilities as a business executive and his work for the NAACP and the Republican Party. [See preceding two items.]

219. Robinson, Lewis Green (1929-   ). *The Making of a Man: An Autobiography.* Illustrated. Cleveland: Green & Sons, 1970. 213p.

DLC   PPiCl   WHi

A lawyer and housing inspector concentrates on his civil rights activities in Cleveland during the 1960s. In addition he depicts his early life in Alabama and Cleveland, his military service in the U.S. Army, his education at Calvin Coolidge College (Boston), Western Reserve University, and the Marshall Law School (Cleveland), and his various jobs in Boston and Cleveland.

220. Robinson, Ray [formerly, Smith, Walker, Jr.] (1921-   ), with Dave Anderson. *Sugar Ray.* Appendix. New York: Viking Press, 1970. 376p. Reprinted New York: Signet Books—New American Library, 1971.

CtH   DHU   DLC   LN   PPi

The former middleweight boxing champion of the world tells the story of his career and his private life, alluding as well to his youth in Detroit and Harlem.

221. Robinson, W[illiam] H. (b. 1848). *From Log Cabin to Pulpit; or Fifteen Years in Slavery.* Illustrated. Eau Claire, Wis.: James H. Tifft, 1913. 200p.

DHU   WE

A former slave in North Carolina and Virginia, Robinson fought for both the Confederate and Union Armies during the Civil War, settling after the conflict in Nashville, where he became a fireman. He later was a singer and banjo player, performing in England. Following his education at Central Tennessee College, he taught school in Tennessee, worked as a railroad porter, served on a Great Lakes steamship, and was a cook in Chicago. His autobiography also covers his religious conversion in 1877 and his evangelical work in the Midwest as both a Baptist and an African Methodist Episcopal preacher and circuit pastor.

222. Russell, Cazzie Lee, Jr. (1944-   ). *Me, Cazzie Russell*. Preface by the Publishers. Illustrated. Westwood, N.J.: Fleming H. Revell, 1967. 122p.
      DLC   MB   MiU   N   NNC   NjP
      Focusing on his high school athletic exploits in Chicago, his college athletic successes at the University of Michigan, and his professional basketball career with the New York Knickerbockers, Russell also alludes to his volunteer work for the Baptist Church.

223. Russell, [William] Bill [Felton] (1934-   ). *Go Up for Glory*. As told to William McSweeny. Illustrated. Index. New York: Coward-McCann, 1966. 224p.
      Reprinted New York: Medallion Books—Berkley Publishing Corp., 1966.
      Reprinted New York: Falcon Books—Noble & Noble, 1968.
      CtH   DHU   DLC   FTaFA   NN   PLuL   PPi   WHi
      Born in Louisiana and reared in Oakland, California, Russell also delineates his basketball career at the University of San Francisco and as a professional with the Boston Celtics.

224. Rutland, Eva (1917-   ). *The Trouble with Being a Mama*. New York: Abingdon Press, 1964. 143p.
      DLC   FTaFA   NN   PLuL   PPiU   WHi   WU
      The author describes her life as a housewife and mother of four children, in Tuskegee, Alabama, Xenia, Ohio, and Sacramento, California. She offers in addition many observations on racial issues, topics, and incidents.

225. Sample, [John] Johnny (1937-   ), with Fred J. Hamilton and Sonny Schwartz. *Confessions of a Dirty Ballplayer*. Foreword by Joe Willie Namath. Illustrated. New York: Dial Press, 1970. 343p.
      Reprinted New York: Dell, 1971.
      CtH   DLC   PPi   WHi
      Devoting most of his book to an account of his career as a professional football player for the Baltimore Colts, Pittsburgh Steelers, Washington Redskins, and New York Jets, Sample also mentions his youth in Virginia and his student days at Maryland State College.

226. Sams, Jessie Bennett (1917-   ). *White Mother*. New York: McGraw-Hill, 1957. 241p.
      DHU   DLC   NN   PPi   PPiU
      A school teacher in Los Angeles touchingly describes the financial

assistance and moral support given her and her sister by a white woman during their youth in Florida. By this and other aid she was eventually to become a graduate of the Florida Agricultural and Mechanical College.

227. Sayers, Gale (1943-   ), with Al Silverman. *I Am Third*. Introduction by Bill Cosby. Illustrated. Appendix. New York: Viking Press, 1970. 238p.

Reprinted New York: Bantam Books, 1972.

CtH   DLC   PPi   RP   WHi

Sayers depicts his early life in Kansas and Omaha, his college years at the University of Kansas, and his professional football career with the Chicago Bears.

228. Schuyler, George Samuel (1895-   ). *Black and Conservative: The Autobiography of George S. Schuyler*. Index. New Rochelle, N.Y.: Arlington House, 1966. 362p.

CSdS   DHU   DLC   FTaFA   N   PLuL   PPi   PPiU   WU

Born in Providence and reared in Syracuse, New York, Schuyler served in the U.S. Army before his distinguished career as a journalist, essayist, fiction writer, and political figure. His autobiography also outlines his conservative political and economic philosophy. [See next item and Item 390.]

229. Schuyler, Philippa Duke (1932-1967). *Adventures in Black and White*. Foreword by Deems Taylor. Illustrated. Index. New York: Robert Speller & Sons, 1960. 302p.

CtY   LU   MiU   NIC   NcD   NcRR   OOxM   PLuL   PP   TxU

George Samuel Schuyler's daughter, herself a pianist and classical-music composer, draws upon her diary entries from 1950 to 1960 to divulge the private and professional experiences of her world travels. [See preceding item and Item 390.]

230. Seale, Bobby G. (1936-   ). *Seize the Time: The Story of the Black Panther Party and Huey P. Newton*. New York: Random House, 1970. 429p.

Reprinted New York: Vintage Books—Random House, 1970.

CU   CoU   GU   IaU   InU   KyU   MiU   NcU   NjR   PPiCl

Seale devotes the major part of his quasi-political autobiography to describing his activities as a leader in the Black Panther Party after 1965, particularly in Berkeley and Oakland, California. He also includes an account of his trial and imprisonment for allegedly trying to disrupt the National Convention of the Democratic Party at Chicago in 1968. Portrayed as well are his early life in Texas and California, his education at Merritt College (Oakland, California), and his military service in the U.S. Air Force.

231. Sellers, Cleveland (1944-   ), with Robert Terrell. *The River of No Return: The Autobiography of a Black Militant and the Life and*

Death of SNCC. Index. New York: William Morrow, 1973. 279p.
DLC PPi PPiCl PPiU

Sellers concentrates on his civil rights activities for the Student Non-violent Coordinating Committee, some of which caused threats on his life to be made, during the period 1962-1968. His work carried him to such places as Mississippi; Cambridge, Maryland; Selma, Alabama; Orangeburg, South Carolina; and Atlanta. He also extensively reviews his youth in Denmark, South Carolina, alludes to his education at Howard University and Harvard University, and mentions his teaching duties at Cornell University.

232. Sewing, Henry Warren (1891-   ). *Henry Warren Sewing; Founder of the Douglass State Bank: An Autobiography*. Illustrated. New York: Exposition Press, 1971. 137p.

DLC PPiCl WHi

A Kansas City, Kansas, businessman, banker, civic leader, NAACP activist, and Baptist Church volunteer elaborates on these roles and on his early life in Texas, his education at Tillotson College (Texas) and Fisk University, as well as his teaching years in Texas schools and at Western University (Kansas).

233. Short, [Robert] Bobby [Waltrip] (1924-   ). *Black and White Baby*. Illustrated. New York: Dodd, Mead, 1971.304p.

Reprinted New York: Curtis Books, 1971.

DLC PPi WU

The autobiography of the popular piano player and singer encompasses his years as a child and a teenager, primarily in Danville, Illinois, and on tours as a young performer.

234. Simpson, O[renthal] J[ames] (1948-   ), with Pete Axthelm. *O. J.: The Education of a Rich Rookie*. Illustrated. New York: Macmillan, 1970. 255p.

CtH DHU DLC NN PPi WHi

Reporting in detail his first year as a professional football player for the Buffalo Bills, Simpson in addition briefly discusses his early life in San Francisco and his athletic career at San Francisco State College and the University of Southern California.

235. Singleton, George Arnett (1896-1970). *The Autobiography of George A. Singleton*. Foreword by John D. Bright, Sr. Illustrated. Appendix. Index. Boston: Forum Publishing Co., 1964. 272p.

CLU DLC ICU MsU NIC NN NNC WHi

Born and reared in South Carolina, Singleton was educated at Allen University, Boston University, the University of Chicago, and Harvard University. He entered the U.S. Army in 1912, serving as a Chaplain, before teaching at Allen University and West Kentucky Industrial College. His African Methodist Episcopal Church work in Massachusetts, South Carolina, Kentucky, Illinois, and Iowa was followed by his editorship of church journals published in Philadelphia, and his efforts as an essayist. He also was president of Paul Quinn College (Texas), and held deanships at Shorter College (Arkansas) and Morris Brown College.

236. Skinner, [Thomas] Tom (1942-   ). *Black and Free*. Illustrated. Grand Rapids, Mich.: Zondervan Publishing House, 1968. 154p.

Reprinted New York: Pyramid Books, 1970.

DHU   DLC   PPi   PPiU   WvU

A young evangelical preacher traces his progress from petty crimes with Harlem street gangs to preaching throughout the U.S. and on the radio.

237. Smith, Amanda Berry (1837-1915). *The Story of the Lord's Dealings with Mrs. Amanda Smith, the Colored Evangelist; Containing an Account of Her Life Work of Faith, and Her Travels in America, England, Ireland, Scotland, India and Africa, as an Independent Missionary: An Autobiography*. Introduction by J. M. Thoburn. Illustrated. Chicago: Meyer & Brother, 1893. 506p.

Reprinted Northbrook, Ill.: Metro Books, 1969.

DHU   DLC   N   PLuL   PPiU   ViHaI   WHi

Born a slave in Maryland, this African Methodist Episcopal evangelist, faith healer, and missionary concentrates on her religious activities in such areas as Philadelphia, New York City, the Northeast, the British Isles, India, and Africa.

238. Smith, David (b. 1784). *Biography of Rev. David Smith, of the A.M.E. Church; Being a Complete History Embracing Over Sixty Years' Labor in the Advancement of the Redeemer's Kingdom on Earth. Including "The History of the Origin and Development of Wilberforce University."* Xenia, Ohio: Xenia Gazette Office, 1881. 135p.

Reprinted Freeport, N.Y.: Books for Libraries Press, 1971.

DHU   NN   NcD   OWibfU   PPiU

A Maryland ex-slave and an African Methodist Episcopal minister in the Xenia, Ohio, area narrates the story of his life and his church work in Philadelphia, New Orleans, Connecticut, New Jersey, and Ohio. The essay about Wilberforce University is by Daniel Payne.

239. Smith, Harry (b. 1815). *Fifty Years of Slavery in the United States of America*. Illustrated. Grand Rapids, Mich.: West Michigan Printing Co., 1891. 183p.

DLC   LU   MiD   N   WvU

In his third-person narrative, the author delves extensively into his slave life in Kentucky and offers vignettes of the lives of other slaves. He concludes with an account of his various jobs and business ventures in Indianapolis and in Michigan.

240. Smith, Homer (1908-   ). *Black Man in Red Russia: A Memoir*. Introduction by Harrison Salisbury. Illustrated. Index. Chicago: Johnson

Publishing Co., 1964. 221p.

CtH   DHU   DLC   FTaFA   NN   NcSalL   PLuL   PPiU   WU

A graduate of the University of Minnesota depicts his life as a foreign correspondent in the USSR from 1932 to 1946, focusing particularly on his World War II experiences and on Soviet attitudes toward black peoples.

241.   Smith, James Lindsey (? -1883?). *Autobiography of James L. Smith, Including, Also, Reminiscences of Slave Life, Recollections of the War, Education of Freedmen, Causes of the Exodus, Etc.* Illustrated. Norwich, Conn.: Press of the Bulletin Co., 1881. 150p.

Reprinted Miami, Fla.: Mnemosyne Publishing Co., 1969.

Reprinted New York: Negro Universities Press, 1970.

Reprinted in *Five Black Lives: The Autobiographies of Venture Smith, James Mars, William Grimes, the Rev. G. W. Offley, James L. Smith*. Middletown, Conn.: Wesleyan Univ. Press, 1971. Pp. 139-240.

CtHT   DHU   DLC   FTaFA   NN   PPiU   ViHaI   WHi   WvU

A shoemaker and Methodist minister in Norwich, Connecticut, describes his slave life in Virginia, his escape to New England in 1838, and his experiences as a freeman.

242.   Smith, Walker, Jr.—see Robinson, Ray.

243.   Smith, William—see Thomas, Will.

244.   Smith, [William] Willie the Lion [Henry Joseph Bonaparte Bertholoff] (1897-1973), with George Hoefer. *Music on My Mind: The Memoirs of an American Pianist*. Foreword by Duke Ellington. Interchapters by George Hoefer. Appendixes. Discography. Index. Garden City, N.Y.: Doubleday, 1964. 318p.

DHU   DLC   FTaFA   NN   PLuL   PPi   WU   WvU

A famous Harlem piano player and jazz-blues composer briefly portrays his early life in Goshen, New York, and Newark, New Jersey, before focusing on his music career.

245.   Somerville, John Alexander (1882-   ). *Man of Color, an Autobiography: A Factual Report on the Status of the American Negro Today*. Preface by Willis O. Tyler. Los Angeles: Lorrin L. Morrison, 1949. 170p.

DHU   FTaFA   NN   NcD   OTU   PLuL   PP   OClJC   ViHaI   WHi

Occasionally inserting essays on racial topics into his account of his life, a Los Angeles dentist, reared in Jamaica and educated at the University of Southern California Dental College, describes his career, his business and political activities, and his work for the NAACP.

246.   Spellman, Cecil Lloyd (1906-   ). *Rough Steps on My Stairway: The Life History of a Negro Educator*. New York: Exposition Press, 1953. 273p.

DHU   FTaFA   MH   NN   NcRR   PLuL   PPiU   TU   TxU   ViHaI

The life story of a college educator and administrator covers his

North Carolina childhood, his studies at the North Carolina Agricultural and Technical College, Oregon State University, and Cornell University, and his teaching and administrative duties at such institutions as the Florida Agricultural and Mechanical College, Bishop College, and the South Carolina Agricultural and Mechanical College.

247. Stallworth, Dave (1941-   ), with R. Conrad Stein. *Look to the Light Side*. Illustrated. Chicago: Open Door Books—Childrens Press, 1970. 62p.

     DLC   PPi

     In a book for young readers, a professional basketball player briefly portrays his youth in Dallas, his college years at Wichita State University, his career with the New York Knickerbockers, the heart attack which threatened his life and career, his recovery, and his return to professional basketball.

248. Starks, John Jacob (1876-1944). *Lo These Many Years: An Autobiographical Sketch*. Introduction by C. A. Johnson. Illustrated. Columbia, S.C.: State Co., 1941. 173p.

     DLC

     Starks was a Baptist minister, a professor, and a college administrator in Georgia and South Carolina. He was born and reared in South Carolina and was graduated from the Atlanta Baptist Institute (now Morehouse College). His autobiography describes his youth, his education, his teaching years in Georgia, his efforts to found the Seneca Institute, and his tenures as president of Morris College and Benedict College.

249. Stevens, Walter James (b. 1877). *Chip on My Shoulder: Autobiography of Walter J. Stevens*. Boston: Meador Publishing Co., 1946. 315p.

     CSdS   DHU   DLC   FTaFA   NN   PPiU   WHi   WvU

     Carrying the account of his life to about 1930, the Harvard-educated author writes of his youth in Boston, his combat service for the U.S. Army during the Spanish-American War, his business and civic activities in Harlem during the 1920s, and his employment in Syracuse by the New York Civil Service. He was also a professional photographer.

250. Steward, Theophilus Gould (1843-1924). *From 1864 to 1914, Fifty Years in the Gospel Ministry; Twenty-Seven Years in the Pastorate; Sixteen Years' Active Service as Chaplain in the U.S. Army; Seven Years Professor in Wilberforce University; Two Trips to Europe; a Trip to Mexico*. Introduction by Reverdy C. Ransom. Illustrated. Philadelphia: A.M.E. Book Concern, 1921. 520p.

     DHU   NN   NjR   OWibfU

     Though not portraying his youth, Steward does select a soundly descriptive title for his book to outline his labors for the African Methodist Episcopal Church in such places as South Carolina, Georgia, Delaware, Philadelphia, Baltimore, and Washington, D.C.; his military service in Colorado, Nebraska, Texas, and the Philippines; his teaching career at Wilberforce University; and his travels in Europe and Mexico. He was in addition an essayist and scholar.

251. Still, James (b. 1812). *Early Recollections and Life of Dr. James Still.* Appendix. Philadelphia: Lippincott, 1877. 274p.

Reprinted Westport, Conn.: Negro Universities Press, 1970.

Reprinted Freeport, N.Y.: Books for Libraries Press, 1971.

Reprinted Medford, N.J.: Medford Historical Society, 1971.

DHU DLC NN NcSalL NjR PPiU TNF WHi

A self-taught New Jersey physician interlaces his autobiography with home remedies and some of his poems.

252. Stroyer, Jacob (1846-1908). *Sketches of My Life in the South.* Introductions by Henry K. Oliver and E. C. Bolles. Salem, Mass.: Salem Press, 1879. 51p.

Reprinted as *My Life in the South.* Salem, Mass.: Newcomb & Gaus, 1898.

Reprinted in *Five Slave Narratives: A Compendium.* New York: Arno Press, 1968.

DHU DLC NN NjP PPiU ViHaI WHi

An African Methodist Episcopal minister in Salem, Massachusetts, narrates the conditions of his slave life in South Carolina until the close of the Civil War.

253. Tarry, Ellen (1906-   ). *The Third Door: The Autobiography of an American Negro Woman.* New York: McKay, 1955. 304p.

Reprinted Westport, Conn.: Negro Universities Press, 1971.

DHU MB NN NcD NcU PLuL PP PPi TU WHi

Prominent as a writer of children's stories, Tarry was born and reared in Birmingham, Alabama, and was educated in a Roman Catholic convent school. She later became a teacher, then a journalist in Birmingham and in New York City, where she was also active in Harlem's interracial Friendship House. She founded a similar institution in Chicago, and voluntarily served many Catholic organizations. During World War II she worked for the U.S.O.

254. Taylor, Marshall William "Major" (1878-1937). *The Fastest Bicycle Rider in the World: The Story of a Colored Boy's Indomitable Courage and Success Against Great Odds.* Illustrated. Worcester, Mass.: Wormley Publishing Co., 1928. 431p.

Abbreviated and reprinted Brattleboro, Vt.: Stephen Greene Press, 1972.

Reprinted Freeport, N.Y.: Books for Libraries Press, 1972.

DLC NN PPiU WHi

Using newspaper clippings to supplement his account of his exploits as a professional bicycle racer, Taylor focuses on the period from 1898 to 1904, as he traveled through the U.S., Europe, Australia, and New Zealand. His autobiography also includes some of his poems, and

alludes to his early life in Indianapolis, as well as his adult life in
Worcester, Massachusetts.

255. Taylor, Susie King (b. 1848). *Reminiscences of My Life in Camp with
the 33d United States Colored Troops Late 1st S.C. Volunteers.* Introduction by Thomas Wentworth Higginson. Illustrated. Appendix.
Boston: The Author, 1902. 82p.
    Reprinted New York: Arno Press, 1968.
    CSdS DHU MiU NIC NN NjR OTU PLuL PPiU WHi
    The author recalls her slave life in Georgia, her escape, her varied
activities with the First South Carolina Volunteers, and her later life
in Boston as a teacher, laundress, and nurse.

256. Terrell, Mary Eliza Church (1863-1954). *A Colored Woman in a White
World.* Preface by H. G. Wells. Index. Washington: Ransdell, 1940.
437p.
    CtY DHU DLC NN NcD OCl OU PLuL PPT ViHaI
    The first president of the National Association of Colored Women,
also active in the NAACP and the Republican Party and a leader in
the women's suffrage movement, Terrell outlines her participation in
these organizations. She writes too of her childhood in Memphis and
Ohio, her teaching experiences at Wilberforce University and in Washington, D.C., her studies in France and Germany, her public lectures,
and her work as a journalist.

257. Thomas, Jesse O. (1885-   ). *My Story in Black and White: The Auto-
biography of Jesse O. Thomas.* Foreword by Whitney M. Young, Jr.
Index. New York: Exposition Press, 1967. 300p.
    DLC PLuL PPiU WU
    Born and reared in Mississippi and educated at Tuskegee Institute,
Thomas tells also of his duties as principal of Voorhees Institute
(South Carolina), as field secretary of the National Urban League, as
an administrator for both the U.S. Government and the American Red
Cross, and as an active participant in Atlanta community affairs during
his retirement years.

258. Thomas, Will [pseud. for Smith, William] (1905-   ). *The Seeking.*
Introduction by Dorothy Canfield Fisher. New York: A. A. Wyn,
1953. 290p.
    DHU FTaSU MB NN NcD OO PLuL PP PPiU ViU
    A fiction writer depicts his life in Chicago, Kansas City, and Los
Angeles, before stressing his experiences as a resident of a Vermont
village after 1946.

259. Thompson, Era Bell. *American Daughter.* Chicago: Univ. of Chicago
Press, 1946. 301p.
    CtH DHU DLC FTaFA NN PLuL PPiU WHi WU WvU
    An editor for *Ebony* magazine portrays her early life in Iowa and
North Dakota, her education at Dawn College (Iowa), her various jobs

in North Dakota and Minnesota, her work in government in Chicago, and her career as a journalist. [See Item 399.]

260. Tunnell, Emlen (1925-   ), with William Gleason. *Footsteps of a Giant.* Appendix. Garden City, N.Y.: Doubleday, 1966. 238p.

  DHU DLC NN PLuL PPi

  An athlete concentrates on his careers, first as a basketball and football player at the University of Toledo, then as a football player at the University of Iowa, and finally as a football professional for the New York Giants and the Green Bay Packers. He alludes as well to his youth in a Philadelphia suburb and to his military service for the U.S. Coast Guard during World War II.

261. Turner, Bridges Alfred (1908-   ). *From a Plow to a Doctorate—So What!* Illustrated. Appendix. Hampton, Va.: The Author, 1945. 89p.

  DLC NN NcD

  Turner portrays his youth in Mississippi and Arkansas; his education at the Arkansas Agricultural, Mechanical and Normal College and at Pennsylvania State College, his experiences as a school teacher in Arkansas, and his professorial duties at Hampton Institute. He further presents his plan for pooling the financial resources of Negroes for business investments and college scholarships.

262. Turner, Robert Emanuel (b. 1875). *Memories of a Retired Pullman Porter.* Appendix. New York: Exposition Press, 1954. 191p.

  DHU DLC NN NcD NcRR PP PU WHi

  A retired railroad porter, working out of Chicago after 1920, narrates his experiences and sketches his earlier life in Atlanta, St. Paul, and Minneapolis.

263. Turnor, Mae Caesar (1889-   ). *Memory Lane in My Southern World.* New York: Vantage Press, 1968. 136p.

  DHU TU

  A professional writer, retired from singing and a teaching career in Oklahoma, writes in detail of her childhood and adolescence in Ennis, Texas.

264. Turpeau, David Dewitt, Sr. (1874-1947). *Up from the Cane-Brakes: An Autobiography.* Cincinnati: The Author, 1942. 43p.

  WHi

  The author was born and reared in Louisiana, worked in New York State, was graduated from Bennett College, and served as a Methodist minister in such places as New York State, New Jersey, Baltimore, West Virginia, Pittsburgh, and Cincinnati. He was active in Republican Party affairs and was elected to the General Assembly of the Ohio Legislature.

265. Veney, Bethany (b. 1815). *The Narrative of Bethany Veney, a Slave Woman.* Introduction by W. A. Mallalieu. Commendatory Notices by Eratus Spaulding and V. A. Cooper. Worcester, Mass.: Press of

George H. Ellis, 1889. 46p.

NN

Veney focuses on her slave life in Virginia, before describing her purchase by a Northerner and her subsequent life in Providence and Worcester, Massachusetts.

266. Walker, Thomas Calhoun (1862-1953). *The Honey-Pod Tree: The Life Story of Thomas Calhoun Walker*. As narrated to Florence L. Lattimore. New York: John Day, 1958. 320p.

CtY   DHU   ICU   IaU   MH   MnU   NjP   PPi   ViU   WaU

A former slave, later educated at Hampton Institute, and then a lawyer, local politician, civic leader, and U.S. Government administrator, narrates his life in Virginia.

267. Walters, Alexander (1858-1917). *My Life and Work*. Introduction by John Edward Bruce. Illustrated. New York: Fleming H. Revell, 1917. 272p.

DHU   DLC   IEG   MB   NN

Walters was born a slave in Kentucky. After the Civil War, he worked in hotels in Louisville and Indianapolis before becoming first a minister in the African Methodist Episcopal Zion Church and later a bishop. His church duties were executed in such places as Louisville, Knoxville, Chattanooga, San Francisco, and New York City. His autobiography also describes his trips to Europe, the Middle East, and Africa and contains a selection of his sermons, addresses, and letters.

268. Ward, Matthew (1907-   ). *Indignant Heart*. New York: New Books, 1952. 184p.

DHU   DLC   NN   NcD   WHi   WvU

A Detroit auto worker active in union organizations, and once a member of the Trotskyist Party, depicts his experiences in the factory, his childhood in Tennessee, and his job as a chauffeur for a prominent Memphis lawyer from 1936 to 1943.

269. Washington, Booker Taliaferro (1856-1915). *The Story of My Life and Work*. Introduction by J. L. M. Curry. Illustrated. Naperville, Ill.: J. L. Nichols & Co., 1900. 423p.

Revised and reprinted Naperville, Ill.: J. L. Nichols & Co., 1901.
Revised and reprinted Naperville, Ill.: J. L. Nichols & Co., 1915.
Reprinted New York: Negro Universities Press, 1969.
Reprinted in *The Booker T. Washington Papers*. Vol. 1, *The Autobiographical Writings*. Edited by Louis R. Harlan et al. Urbana: Univ. of Illinois Press, 1972. Pp. 3-206.

DHU   DLC   FTaFA   NN   PLuL   PPiCl   PPiU   TNF   ViHal   WvU

The famous racial spokesman and the first principal of the Tuskegee Normal and Industrial Institute portrays his slave life in Virginia, his boyhood in West Virginia, his education at Hampton Institute, and his work at Tuskegee. [See next two items and Items 404 and 405.]

270. Washington, Booker Taliaferro (1856-1915). *Up from Slavery: An Autobiography*. Illustrated. New York: Doubleday, Page, 1901. 330p.
    Reprinted Garden City, N.Y.: Sun Dial Press, 1937.
    Reprinted Garden City, N.Y.: Doubleday, 1953.
    Reprinted New York: Bantam Books, 1956.
    Reprinted in *Three Negro Classics*. Edited by John Hope Franklin. New York: Avon Books, 1956. Pp. 29-205.
    Reprinted Boston: Western Islands Publisher, 1965.
    Reprinted New York: Dodd, Mead, 1965.
    Reprinted New York: Airmont Classics, 1967.
    Reprinted Boston: Houghton Mifflin, 196?.
    Reprinted New York: Limited Editions Club, 1970.
    Reprinted Williamstown, Mass.: Corner House, 1971.
    Reprinted in *The Booker T. Washington Papers*. Vol. 1, *The Autobiographical Writings*. Edited by Louis R. Harlan et al. Urbana: Univ. of Illinois Press, 1972, Pp. 209-385.
    CtY DHU NN NNC NcU PPiCl RP TNF WaU WvU
    The first principal of Tuskegee Institute uses a more literary style to recount the story he had told in his first autobiography. [See preceding item, next item, and Items 404 and 405.]
271. Washington, Booker Taliaferro (1856-1915). *My Larger Education: Being Chapters from My Experience*. Illustrated. New York: Doubleday, Page, 1911. 313p.
    Reprinted Miami, Fla.: Mnemosyne Publishing Co., 1969.
    CSdS DHU DLC NcSalL PLuL PPiU WHi WU WvU
    This unchronological account of portions of his life further elaborates Washington's experiences as principal of Tuskegee Institute. [See preceding two items and Items 404 and 405.]
272. Washington, Kipp [pseud.]. *Some Like It Dark: The Intimate Autobiography of a Negro Call Girl*. As told to Leo Guild. Los Angeles: Holloway House, 1966. 223p.
    IU
    The author's story begins in Brooklyn when she was fifteen. The professional criminal activities she vividly describes here occurred primarily in New York City, Las Vegas, and Miami, Florida.
273. Washington, Vivian Edwards (1914-   ). *Mount Ascutney*. New York: Comet Press Books, 1958. 66p.
    DHU DLC N NN NcRR WHi
    Most of this book depicts the author's childhood and adolescence in Claremont, New Hampshire. She does briefly mention her education at Howard University and her positions as a teacher, school counselor, and social worker in Baltimore.
274. Waters, Ethel (1896-   ), with Charles Samuels. *His Eye Is on the*

Sparrow: An Autobiography. Garden City, N.Y.: Doubleday, 1951. 278p.

Reprinted New York: Pyramid Books, 1967.

DHU DLC FTaFA NN PLuL PPi PPiCl PPiU WU WvU

A singer and actress follows a long account of her youth in the Chester, Pennsylvania, area with descriptions of the important events in her career. [See next item.]

275. Waters, Ethel (1896-   ). *To Me It's Wonderful*. Introduction by Eugenia Price and Joyce Blackburn. Illustrated. New York: Harper & Row, 1972. 162p.

DLC   PPi   PPiCl   PPiU

Continuing her life story after 1957, the author mentions certain events in her career as a gospel singer, especially with the Billy Graham Crusade. She occasionally flashes back to her childhood years. [See preceding item.]

276. Wayman, Alexander Walker (1821-1895). *My Recollections of African M.E. Ministers, or Forty Years' Experience in the African Methodist Episcopal Church*. Introduction by B. T. Tanner. Philadelphia: A.M.E. Book Rooms, 1881. 250p.

DHU   DLC   NN   WHi

Merely alluding to his childhood in Maryland, a bishop in the African Methodist Episcopal Church tells of his ministerial labors, notably in Philadelphia, Baltimore, and Washington, D.C.

277. Webb, William (b. 1836). *The History of William Webb, Composed by Himself*. Illustrated. Detroit: Egbert Hoekstra, 1873. 77p.

DLC

Before serving with the Union Army during the Civil War, the author had been a slave in Georgia, Mississippi, and Kentucky. He later worked at odd jobs in the Midwest, particularly in St. Louis, Indianapolis, and Detroit, where he finally settled.

278. Wells [Barnett], Ida B. (1862-1931). *Crusade for Justice: The Autobiography of Ida B. Wells*. Edited and Introduction by Alfreda M. Duster. Foreword by John Hope Franklin. Illustrated. Bibliography. Index. Chicago: Univ. of Chicago Press, 1970. 434p.

DLC   PPi   PPiCl   PPiU   WU   WvU

A noted civil rights worker and civic leader who was born a slave in Mississippi, the author later became a teacher in Memphis before moving to Chicago. She played a prominent role in NAACP activities and was also a journalist and newspaper editor. Her autobiography, edited by her daughter, carries her life through 1921, with one chapter devoted to events in 1927.

279. White, Charley C. (1885-   ), and Ada Morehead Holland. *No Quittin' Sense*. Foreword by Ada Morehead Holland. Illustrated. Austin: Univ.

of Texas Press, 1969. 216p.

DHU   DLC   ICU   NN   PPi   PPiU   WU   WvU

Written in an informal and vernacular style, the recollections of a former Texas farmer and Baptist minister in Jacksonville, Texas, begin in 1928.

280. White, Walter Francis (1893-1955). *A Man Called White: The Autobiography of Walter White*. Index. New York: Viking Press, 1948. 382p.

Reprinted New York: Arno Press, 1969.

Reprinted Bloomington: Indiana Univ. Press, 1970.

CSdS   DHU   FTaSU   NN   NSyU   OTU   PLuL   PPiCl   PPiU   WU

The essayist, novelist, lecturer, and long-time secretary of the NAACP, born and reared in Atlanta and educated at Atlanta University, concentrates on his distinguished career as a national civil rights leader and organizer.

281. Whitmore, Terry (1947-   ). *Memphis Nam Sweden: The Autobiography of a Black American Exile*. As told to and Foreword by Richard Weber. Garden City, N.Y.: Doubleday, 1971. 189p.

DLC   PPiU   WHi   WU   WvU

A former U.S. Marine portrays his youth in Memphis, his combat service during the Vietnam War, and his expatriate life in Sweden after a brief visit to the USSR.

282. Williams, Billy Leo (1938-   ), with Rick Simon. *Iron Man*. Illustrated. Chicago: Open Door Books—Childrens Press, 1970. 64p.

DLC

In a short volume for young readers, a professional baseball player treats his youth in the Mobile, Alabama, area, his apprenticeship with minor league professional teams, and the early stages of his career with the Chicago Cubs.

283. Williams, G[ladnil] Bernell (1893-   ). *Look Not Upon Me Because I Am Black*. New York: Carlton Press, 1970. 78p.

IU

After spending his youth in Michigan, Wisconsin, and Cleveland, Williams worked at various jobs in Bloomington, Indiana, and Lansing, Michigan. He later was graduated from Michigan State University and then sold insurance, was a civil servant, and taught school. His autobiography also covers his community activities, civil rights work, and duties for the African Methodist Episcopal Church. For many years he was employed by the Michigan Tuberculosis Association. Included in his volume are some of his essays and poems.

284. Williams, Isaac D. (1821-1898). *Sunshine and Shadow of Slave Life: Reminiscences as Told by Isaac D. Williams to "Tege."* East Saginaw, Mich.: Evening News Printing & Binding House, 1885. 91p.

DHU   DLC   MB   NN

A short account of Williams' jobs as a laborer in Canada and Michigan is preceded by an extensive commentary on his slave life in Virginia and his escape to Canada in 1858 through the Underground Railroad.

285. Williams, James (b. 1825). *Life and Adventures of James Williams, a Fugitive Slave, with a Full Description of the Underground Railroad.* San Francisco: Women's Union Print, 1873. 108p.

Reprinted Philadelphia: Rhistoric Publications, 1969.
Reprinted San Francisco: R & E Research Associates, 1969.
DLC   NN   PPiCl   WHi

Featuring lengthy descriptions of the author's slave life in Maryland, his escape to Pennsylvania in 1838, and his work for the Underground Railroad, this narrative also covers Williams' experiences as a California gold miner, a businessman in California and Nevada, and a worker for the African Methodist Episcopal Church in Sacramento. Also included are vignettes of other slaves known by the author.

286. Williams, James H. (1864-1927). *Blow the Man Down! An Autobiographical Narrative Based Upon the Writings of James H. Williams.* Arranged, edited, and Preface by Warren F. Kuehl. Illustrated. Bibliography. Glossary. New York: Dutton, 1959. 255p.

CtY   DHU   IaU   LU   MH   NIC   NNC   NjP   NjR   WaU

Williams left his Fall River, Massachusetts, home at the age of twelve to become a sailor. He later was active in the seamen's labor movement. His autobiography also describes his adventures and work around the world.

287. Williams, Rose Berthenia Clay (1910-   ). *Black and White Orange: An Autobiography.* New York: Vantage Press, 1961. 135p.

DHU   FTaFA   N

A Florida teacher portrays her youth in Tampa, her education at the Florida Agricultural and Mechanical College, and her teaching experiences. Her autobiography also contains her essays on education and teaching, in addition to some of her poems.

288. Williamson, Henry [pseud.] (1930-   ). *Hustler!* Edited and Introduction by R. Lincoln Keiser. Commentary by Paul Bohannan. Garden City, N.Y.: Doubleday, 1965. 222p.

Reprinted New York: Avon Books, 1966.
CtY   GU   IU   N   NN   NNC   NcD   NcU   PLuL   WU

A prison inmate describes his youth in Alabama and Chicago, his criminal activities in Chicago, his struggle to break his narcotics habit, and his experiences in jails.

289. Wright, Richard Nathaniel (1908-1960). *Black Boy: A Record of Childhood and Youth.* New York: Harper & Bros., 1945. 228p.

Reprinted New York: Perennial Classic—Harper & Row, 1966.
CSdS   CtHT   DHU   FTaFA   NN   PLuL   PPiCl   PPiU   WU   WvU

The famous fiction writer, poet, dramatist, and essayist covers his first nineteen years in Mississippi, Arkansas, and Memphis. Included are accounts of his various jobs and of his petty criminal activities. [See Items 413, 414, 415, 416, and 417.]

290. Wright, Richard Robert, Jr. (1878-1967). *87 Years Behind the Black Curtain: An Autobiography*. Index. Philadelphia: Rare Book Co., 1965. 351p.

CtY   DHU   DLC   FTaFA   NjP   NjR   PLuL

Born and reared in Georgia, and educated at Georgia State College, the University of Chicago, and the University of Pennsylvania, Wright became a minister in the African Methodist Episcopal Church, preaching in Chicago and Philadelphia, where he also was a social worker. He twice was president of Wilberforce University and was named a church bishop, serving in Africa, the West Indies, Tennessee, Kentucky, Georgia, Mississippi, Louisiana, and the Far West. Wright was also a scholar, sociologist, essayist, editor, and lecturer, and his autobiography portrays his diverse activities. [See Item 412.]

291. Yancey, [Arthur] Asa Henry (1881-   ). *Interpositionulification: What the Negro May Expect*. Illustrated. New York: Comet Press Books, 1959. 134p.

CLU   DHU   GU   MoSW   NN   NNC   NcD   WHi

Often using the third person, and frequently inserting comments on racial issues, the author also depicts his childhood in Georgia and his activities in Atlanta as a carpenter, building contractor, and postal worker.

II. Autobiographical books

292. Adams, Effie Kay (1925-). *Experiences of a Fulbright Teacher.* Boston: Christopher Publishing House, 1956. 215p.

     CU   DHU   IU   KU   LU   MB   NN   OkU   PPiU   WU

     The author describes her experiences as an exchange teacher in Pakistan in 1952 and 1953. She also covers her travels in Asia, the Middle East, and Europe.

293. Anderson, Garland (1886-1939). *From Newsboy and Bellhop to Playwright.* San Francisco: The Author, n.d. [1925?]. 30p.

     Reprinted in Anderson's *Uncommon Sense: The Law of Life in Action.* London: L. N. Fowler & Co., 1933. Pp. 60-90.

     CU   RPB

     Primarily an essay on how to become a success, this pamphlet also sketches the author's work as a newsboy and hotel bellhop in San Francisco and the circumstances leading to the production of his play *Appearances* on Broadway in 1925.

294. Anderson, Robert (b. 1819). *The Anderson Surpriser. Written After He Was Seventy-Five Years of Age. This Book Contains an Account of His Florida and Northern Trip, Written by Himself, Giving Much Valuable Information of the People Among Whom He Had Been for Several Months.* Macon, Ga.: The Author, 1895. 112p.

     GU

     A Methodist Episcopal minister from Georgia uses diary like entries to describe his experiences while preaching, traveling, and selling his autobiography in Florida and Northeastern cities in 1893 and 1894. [See Item 7.]

295. Anderson, Rosa Claudette. *River, Face Homeward (Suten Dan Wani Hwe Fie): An Afro-American in Ghana.* Illustrated. New York: Exposition Press, 1966. 121p.

     DHU   DLC   PPiU

     An Arizona schoolteacher writes an annecdotal, conversation-filled account of her visit to Ghana.

296. Anthony, Earl (1941-). *Picking Up the Gun: A Report on the Black Panthers.* New York: Dial Press, 1970. 160p.

     Reprinted New York: Pyramid Publications, 1971.

     CtY   IU   InU   MB   MiU   N   NcD   PPi   PPiU   WU

     Describing events from Fall 1967 to Spring 1969, the former Deputy Minister of Education in the Black Panther Party treats his activities in California and Japan.

297. Armstrong, Louis (1900-1971), and Richard Meryman. *Louis Armstrong— A Self Portrait.* Illustrated. New York: Eakins Press, 1971. 59p.

DLC   PPiU   WU

Interviews in 1966 with the jazz musician and singer provide a brief running commentary on his youth in New Orleans, and his career, particularly in Chicago and New York City. [See Items 11 and 12.]

298. Bailey, Pearl (1918-   ). *Talking to Myself*. New York: Harcourt Brace Jovanovich, 1971. 233p.

Reprinted New York: Pocket Books, 1973.

DLC   PPi   PPiU

With scattered references to her career and her personal life, especially after 1965, the popular singer and actress reflects on a variety of subjects and issues, some of them racial. She also prints a selection of her poems. [See Item 16.]

299. Baldwin, James (1924-   ). *Notes of a Native Son*. Boston: Beacon Press, 1955. 175p.

Reprinted New York: Dial Press, 1963.

Reprinted New York: Bantam Books, 1964.

CSdS   CU   DHU   FTaSU   NN   OTU   OrU   PLuL   PPiCl   WU

A collection of essays by the prominent novelist, dramatist, and essayist includes references to his experiences in Harlem, Paris, and Switzerland. [See next four items.]

300. Baldwin, James (1924-   ). *Nobody Knows My Name: More Notes of a Native Son*. New York: Dial Press, 1961. 241p.

Reprinted New York: Dell, 1963.

CSdS   DHU   FTaSU   MiU   NN   OTU   PLuL   PPiCl   PPiU   WU

Details of Baldwin's activities in Paris, Harlem, and the South appear in this collection of his essays on racial and literary topics. [See preceding item and next three items.]

301. Baldwin, James (1924-   ). *The Fire Next Time*. New York: Dial Press, 1963. 120p.

Reprinted New York: Dell, 1964.

CSdS   DHU   FTaSU   NN   OTU   PLuL   PPiCl   PPiU   TxU   WU

This personal commentary on American racial attitudes and problems also contains accounts of Baldwin's religious crisis in Harlem when he was fourteen, and of certain of his adult experiences in Chicago. [See preceding two items and next two items.]

302. Baldwin, James (1924-   ), and Margaret Mead. *A Rap on Race*. Philadelphia: Lippincott, 1971. 256p.

Reprinted New York: Delta Books—Dell, 1972.

CSt   CtH   MH   MiEM   MoSW   NN   PPiCl   PPiU   WU   WvU

In tape-recorded discussions on racial problems with a noted anthropologist, Baldwin alludes to many incidents in both his private and public life. [See preceding three items and next item.]

303. Baldwin, James (1924-   ). *No Name in the Street*. New York: Dial Press, 1972. 197p.

Reprinted New York: Delta Books—Dell, 1973.

CtH   DLC   PPi   PPiCl   PPiU   WU   WvU

Baldwin's personal discourses on primarily racial topics are dotted with reminiscences of events in his life in Paris, London, New York City, and California. [See preceding four items.]

304. Baraka, Imamu Amiri—see Jones, LeRoi.
305. Bass, Charlotta A. (1890-1969). *Forty Years: Memoirs from the Pages of a Newspaper*. Illustrated. Los Angeles: The Author, 1960. 198p.

DLC   MH   NN

A journalist, and the owner and editor of a newspaper published at Los Angeles, the *California Eagle*, and the U.S. Vice-Presidential candidate for the Progressive Party in 1948, the author writes on racial and civil rights topics, stressing the role of her newspaper in public events between 1912 and 1951.

306. Bates, Daisy Gatson (1922-   ). *The Long Shadow of Little Rock: A Memoir*. Foreword by Eleanor Roosevelt. Illustrated. Index. New York: McKay, 1962. 234p.

CSdS   DHU   DLC   NN   PLuL   PPi   PPiU   WHi   WU   WvU

As the copublisher of a newspaper, Mrs. Bates describes her struggles to contribute to the racial integration of public schools in Little Rock, Arkansas, during 1957 and after. She also outlines her youth in Arkansas.

307. Beck, Robert [formerly Iceberg Slim] (1918-   ). *The Naked Soul of Iceberg Slim*. Introduction by Milton Van Sickle. Los Angeles: Holloway House, 1971. 248p.

DLC   PPiCl

Beck's essays and letters, often on racial matters, also include information about his earlier criminal activities in Chicago, his experiences in a reform institution, his actual reformation, and his life in Los Angeles. [See Item 23.]

308. Booker, Simeon Saunders (1918-   ). *Black Man's America*. Index. Englewood Cliffs, N.J.: Prentice-Hall, 1964. 230p.

CSdS   DHU   FTaFA   NN   NcSalL   OTU   PLuL   PPiU   WU   WvU

A radio commentator and journalist analyzes racial issues and civil rights problems, sprinkling his book with reports of his personal experiences.

309. Bradford, [John Henry] Perry (1895-1961). *Born with the Blues: Perry Bradford's Own Story*. Foreword by Noble Sissle, Jr. Illustrated. Musical scores. Index. New York: Oak Publications, 1965. 175p.

CSdS   CtH   DHU   DLC   ICU   NN   PLuL   PPiU   WHi

The entertainer, piano player, and jazz-blues composer defends his role in popularizing the blues, while providing glimpses of his youth in Alabama and Atlanta, and of his music career, primarily in Chicago and New York City.

310. Brown, Azariah. *A Life Sketch of King Azariah Brown: Consisting of a Personal Narrative; Remarks on the Church as It Is To-day; the Colored Race; Religion, Temperance, &c.* Appendix. Hudson, N.Y.: The Author, 1898. 69p.

　　DLC

　　In a pamphlet dealing essentially with racial and religious matters, a camp-meeting minister, also a general laborer and farmer, mentions some of his experiences in Connecticut, Massachusetts, and the Hudson, New York, area.

311. Campbell, Thomas Monroe (1883-　). *The Movable School Goes to the Negro Farmer.* Introduction by Bradford Knapp. Illustrated. Appendix. Tuskegee Institute, Ala.: Tuskegee Institute Press, 1936. 170p.

　　Reprinted New York: Arno Press, 1969.

　　AU　DHU　FTaSU　MiU　NN　NcD　OU　PP　PPiU　WHi

　　A field agent in the Extension Service of the U.S. Department of Agriculture, reared in Georgia and educated at Tuskegee Institute, Campbell emphasizes the history, practices, and goals of the educational services offered by his organization, while often alluding to his own life and experiences. [See next item.]

312. Campbell, Thomas Monore (1883-　). *The School Comes to the Farmer: The Autobiography of T. M. Campbell.* Foreword by Jackson Davis. Illustrated. New York: Longmans, Green, 1947. 64p.

　　DHU　DNAL　MiU　N　NIC　NN　PSt

　　This pamphlet is an abridgment of the book earlier published by Campbell. [See preceding item.]

313. Cansler, Charles Warner (1871-1953). *Three Generations: The Story of a Colored Family of Eastern Tennessee.* Illustrated. Kingsport, Tenn.: The Author, 1939. 173p.

　　DHU　NIC　NN　NcD　OCl　PLuL　PP　TU　ViHaI　ViU

　　The first two sections of Cansler's book are vignettes of the two preceding generations of the author's family. In the third section he portrays his childhood in Tennessee, his college years, his employment at odd jobs, and his long career as a teacher and administrator in Knoxville.

314. Carter, Vincent O. (1924-　). *The Bern Book: A Record of a Voyage of the Mind.* Preface by Herbert R. Lottman. New York: John Day, 1973. 297p.

　　DLC　PPiCl

　　An unpublished fiction writer and essayist creates an impressionistic history of himself as an expatriate and portrays the city in which he has resided since 1953, Bern, Switzerland. He also mentions his youth in Kansas City, his brief studies at Oxford University, his U.S. Army service in France during World War II, and his travels in Europe, especially to Paris.

315. Chisholm, Shirley (1924-   ). *The Good Fight*. Appendix. Index. New York: Harper & Row, 1973. 206p.

 DLC   PPiCl

 The U.S. congresswoman from New York City describes her unsuccessful campaign in many states to win the Democratic Party Presidential nomination in 1972. She also outlines her views on various political and racial issues. [See Item 45.]

316. Cleaver, Eldridge (1935-   ). *Soul on Ice*. Introduction by Maxwell Geismar. New York: McGraw-Hill, 1968. 210p.

 Reprinted New York: Delta Books—Dell, 1968.

 Reprinted New York: Dell, 1970.

 CSdS   DHU   FTaSU   MnU   OTU   PLuL   PPiCl   PPiU   WU   WaU

 A leader in the Black Panther Party writes from a California prison about racial and social issues, literary topics, his early life and criminal activities in California, and his prison experiences. [See next two items.]

317. Cleaver, Eldridge (1935-   ). *Post-Prison Writings and Speeches*. Edited and Introduction by Robert Scheer. Appendix. New York: Random House, 1969. 211p.

 Reprinted New York: Vintage Books—Random House, 1969.

 CSdS   CtHT   GU   KU   KyU   NjR   OrU   PPi   PPiU   WU

 Cleaver discusses racial and political topics, and describes his political activities for the Black Panther Party in 1967 and 1968. [See preceding item and next item.]

318. Cleaver, Eldridge (1935-   ), and Lee Lockwood. *Conversation with Eldridge Cleaver*. Introduction by Lee Lockwood. New York: McGraw-Hill, 1970. 131p.

 Reprinted New York: Delta Books—Dell, 1970.

 DHU   DLC   PPi   PPiU   WU

 A fugitive in Algeria, the essayist and revolutionary political leader discourses on political and racial issues, interjecting references to his own life. [See preceding two items.]

319. Cole, Maria Ellington (1926-   ), with Louie Robinson. *Nat King Cole: An Intimate Biography*. Illustrated. Discography. New York: William Morrow, 1971. 184p.

 DLC   PPi   PPiU

 The wife of Nat King Cole, a famous singer, focuses on their life together from 1946 to 1965, often in New York City and Los Angeles. She also portrays her youth in the Boston area and North Carolina, her education at the Boston Clerical College, and her own brief singing career.

319a. Comer, James P. (1933-   ). *Beyond Black and White*. Introduction by Robert Coles. Foreword by Richard Gordon Hatcher. Footnotes. Bibliography. Index. New York: Quadrangle Books, 1972. 272p.

DLC PPi PPiU WvU

A physician, psychiatrist, and U.S. Public Health official analyzes the history of racism and its effects on the mentalities of both whites and blacks. In a brief autobiographical section at the beginning of his book, he sketches his youth in East Chicago, Indiana, and his education at Indiana University and Howard University.

320. Coppin, Fanny M. Jackson (1836-1913). *Reminiscences of School Life, and Hints on Teaching*. Preface by Levi Jenkins Coppin. Illustrated. Philadelphia: A.M.E. Book Concern, 1913. 191p.

DHU MB NN OWibfC WHi

A former teacher in a Philadelphia Quaker school, and the wife of Levi Jenkins Coppin, comments on classroom methodology and provides biographical sketches of certain teachers and students of her school. She also briefly outlines her life as a slave in Washington, D.C.; her purchase by a New England family; her life in New Bedford, Massachusetts, and Newport, Rhode Island; her education at Oberlin College; her teaching career in Philadelphia; and her travels to England and Africa. [See next item and Item 52.]

321. Coppin, Levi Jenkins (1848-1924). *Observations of Persons and Things in South Africa, 1900-1904*. Illustrated. Philadelphia: A.M.E. Book Concern, n.d. [1905?]. 415p.

DHU IEG NN NcD

This African Methodist Episcopal bishop describes his travels in Africa and his religious work there, and includes a collection of his letters from Africa in 1901. [See preceding item and Item 52.]

322. Curtis, George M. *Bellhop Blues*. New York: Carlton Press, 1960. 56p.

CLU CU-A DHU IU

Commenting on a variety of topics, the author also reminisces about his thirty-five years as a hotel bellhop in Omaha, Los Angeles, and Reno, Nevada.

323. Daniel, William Lofton (1895-   ). *My Memories of the Century Club, 1919-1958*. Appendix. N.P. [New York?]: Privately Printed for the Members of the Century Association, 1959. 158p.

CtY DHU NIC

A former employee of an exclusive social club in New York City recalls his experiences in the club and his contacts with members.

324. Du Bois, William Edward Burghardt (1868-1963). *Darkwater: Voices from Within the Veil*. New York: Harcourt, Brace, 1920. 276p.

Reprinted New York: AMS Press, 1969.

Reprinted New York: Schocken Books, 1969.

CtHT DHU FTaFA MB MiU NN NcD PLuL PPiCl PPiU

Many autobiographical references are added to this collection of some of the author's stories, poems, and peripatetic essays. [See next two items and Item 67.]

325. Du Bois, William Edward Burghardt (1868-1963). *Dusk of Dawn: An Essay Toward an Autobiography of Race Concept*. Index. New York: Harcourt, Brace, 1940. 334p.

     Reprinted New York: Schocken Books, 1968.

     CSdS DHU FTaSU NN OTU OrU PLuL PP PPiCl PPiU

     Incorporated into this collection of essays on racial topics are lengthy sketches of Du Bois' youth, education, publishing activities, NAACP work, and foreign travels. [See preceding item, next item, and Item 67.]

326. Du Bois, William Edward Burghardt (1868-1963). *W. E. B. Du Bois Speaks: Speeches and Addresses 1890-1963*. 2 vols. Edited, Introduction to Vol. 1, and Preface to Vol. 2 by Philip S. Foner. Tribute in Vol. 1 by Martin Luther King, Jr. Tribute in Vol. 2 by Kwame Nkrumah. Notes. Indexes. Bibliography. New York: Pathfinder Press, 1970. 289p. and 346p.

     CSt CoU GU InU KU KyU MiU PPiU ViU WU

     Numerous autobiographical references are made in this two-volume collection. [See preceding two items and Item 67.]

327. Dunham, Katherine (1910-   ). *Katherine Dunham's Journey to Accompong*. Introduction by Ralph Linton. Illustrated. New York: Henry Holt, 1946. 162p.

     Reprinted Westport, Conn.: Negro Universities Press, 1972.

     CU DHU FTaFA MH MiU NIC NcD PLuL PPiU ViU

     Dunham publishes a diary like account of her experiences in, and impressions of, a village in Jamaica during a month's field trip in the 1930s, when she was an anthropology student at the University of Chicago. [See next item and Item 68.]

328. Dunham, Katherine (1910-   ). *Island Possessed*. Glossary. Garden City, N.Y.: Doubleday, 1969. 280p.

     DLC PPi PPiU WU

     In a travelogue, memoir, and anthropological study, the author describes her visits to Haiti between 1936 and 1962. [See preceding item and Item 68.]

329. Ellison, Ralph Waldo (1914-   ). *Shadow and Act*. New York: Random House, 1964. 317p.

     Reprinted New York: Signet Books—New American Library, 1966.
     Reprinted New York: Vintage Books—Random House, 1972.

     CSdS DHU FTaSU NN PLuL PPiCl PPiU WHi WU WvU

     In the collection of his essays on literature, music, and racial matters, the fiction writer and university teacher also recalls events of his youth in Oklahoma City, of his collegiate years at Tuskegee Institute, and of his music and literary careers in New York City.

330. Evers, [Myrlie Beasley] Mrs. Medgar (1933-   ), with William Peters. *For Us, the Living*. Garden City, N.Y.: Doubleday, 1967. 378p.

Reprinted New York: Ace Books, 1970.

CSdS DHU DLC NN NcSalL PLuL PPi PPiU WHi WvU

Concentrating on the Mississippi civil rights activities of her husband before his assassination in 1963 and her contributions to them, the author also describes her childhood in Vicksburg, Mississippi, and her education at the Alcorn Agricultural and Mechanical College.

330a. Ferguson, Ira Lunan (1904-   ). *Our Two Ocean Voyages: The Orient and the Mediterranean-Morocco: A Travelogue*. Forewords by Marianus Kengo Ishii and Tadashi Mitsui. Illustrated. San Francisco: Lunan-Ferguson Library, 1968. 317p.

DLC MB PPiCl

Ferguson writes a lengthy remembrance of the vacation tour he and his wife took in Hawaii and Asian countries in 1966. He follows this with a shorter account of their visit to Europe and Morocco in 1967. [See next item and Items 73 and 74.]

331. Ferguson, Ira Lunan (1904-   ). *I Dug Graves at Night to Attend College by Day: Reflections: This West Indian-American Looks Back Over 50 Years of Life in America: Humor—Pathos—Rewards: An Autobiography*. Vol. 3. San Francisco: Lunan-Ferguson Library, 1970. 296p.

CLU CU DLC InU MiU NIC NN NNC NjP PPiCl

A San Francisco psychologist, essayist, and fiction writer discusses many topics, some of them racial, and refers to many experiences in his own life. [See preceding item and Items 73 and 74.]

332. Fields, Alonzo (1900-   ). *My 21 Years in the White House*. Appendix. New York: Coward-McCann, 1961. 223p.

DLC FTaFA NN PP WHi WU

The former chief butler and maître d'hotel at the White House describes some of his experiences during his service in four presidential administrations from 1931, also presenting many anecdotes about significant national and international public figures. He sketches as well his childhood in Indiana, his business activities in Indianapolis, his studies at the New England Conservatory of Music, and his duties as the butler for the president of the Massachusetts Institute of Technology.

333. Fletcher, [Thomas] Tom (1873-1954). *100 Years of the Negro in Show Business: The Tom Fletcher Story*. Illustrated. New York: Burdge & Co., 1954. 337p.

CU DHU FTaSU IU MH MsU NN TxU WHi WaU

A singer, dancer, and comedian alludes to his boyhood in Ohio and his career as an entertainer, while concentrating on the history of the Negro in show business, particularly between 1890 and 1920.

334. Foster, Marcus Albert (1923-1973). *Making Schools Work: Strategies for Changing Education*. Foreword by Alex Haley. Index. Philadelphia: Westminster Press, 1971. 171p.

CtH   DLC   PPi   PPiCl   PPiU   WU

The Superintendent of Schools in Oakland, California, sets down general rules and principles for dealing with problems in urban public education, culling examples from his experiences as a principal in three Philadelphia schools.

335. Fuller, Hoyt William (1927-   ). *Journey to Africa*. Chicago: Third World Press, 1971. 95p.

DLC   PPiCl   PPiU   WU

The journalist and Editor of *Black World* analyzes African problems, while describing his personal experiences in Africa during visits between 1959 and 1970.

336. Fulton, David Bryant—see Thorne, Jack.

337. Gayle, Addison, Jr. (1932-   ). *The Black Situation*. New York: Horizon Press, 1970. 221p.

Reprinted New York: Delta Books—Dell, 1972.

CSt   CoU   GU   IaU   KU   MB   NjR   PPiCl   PPiU   ViU

A professor and scholar examines racial topics and aesthetic questions in literature, often using his own history and experiences as illustrations. Gayle mentions events in his life as they occurred in such places as the University of California, New York City, and Newport News, Virginia, where he grew up.

338. Giovanni, Nikki (1943-   ). *Gemini: An Extended Autobiographical Statement on My First Twenty-Five Years of Being a Black Poet*. Introduction by Barbara Crosby. Illustrated. Indianapolis: Bobbs-Merrill, 1971. 149p.

Reprinted New York: Compass Books—Viking Press, 1973.

CtH   DLC   PPi   PPiCl   PPiU   WU   WvU

These essays by a poet treat a variety of racial and literary matters, while often alluding to the author's family, her early life in Knoxville and a Cincinnati suburb, and her education at Fisk University.

339. Green, John Paterson (1845-1940). *Recollections of the Inhabitants, Localities, Superstitions, and Kuklux Outrages of the Carolinas*. N.P. [Cleveland?]: The Author, 1880. 205p.

Reprinted, microcard, Louisville: Lost Cause Press, 1964.

DLC   MoU   MsU   NN   NcU   NcWsW   OClWHi   TxU   WvU

A study of the political and social climates of North and South Carolina includes personal incidents during the author's travels in those two states in 1872. [See Item 98.]

340. Gregory, Richard Claxton (1932-   ). *The Shadow That Scares Me*. Edited and Introduction by James R. McGraw. Garden City, N.Y.: Doubleday, 1968. 213p.

Reprinted New York: Pocket Books, 1968.

AU   CtY   DHU   KU   KyU   OrU   PLuL   PPiU   WaU   WvU

A comedian, political figure, and civil rights leader here publishes essays on racial issues and topics, often referring to events in his own life. [See Item 99.]

341. Grimke, Francis James (1850-1937). *The Works of Francis J. Grimké: Addresses, Sermons, Thoughts and Meditations, Letters.* 4 vols. Edited and Introductions by Carter G. Woodson. Indexes. Washington: Associated Publishers, 1942. 633p., 604p., 645p., and 592p.

CU   DHU   IU   NN   NcD   OrU   PPiU   ViU   WHi   WvU

Many autobiographical references are found in the collected works of the nationally known civil rights leader and Presbyterian minister in Washington, D.C. [See Item 435.]

342. Hamilton, Jeff (1840-1950?). *"My Master": The Inside Story of Sam Houston and His Times, by His Former Slave.* As told to, and Preface by, Lenoir Hunt. Foreword by Franklin Williams. Illustrated. Bibliography. Notes. Dallas: Manfred, Van Nort & Co., 1940. 141p.

DHU   DLC   NN   NcD   NcU   OU   TxU

A former servant of the famous Texas general, U.S. senator, and governor concentrates on Houston's duties and adventures in Texas from 1840 to 1863. Hamilton also briefly portrays his childhood as a slave in Kentucky and Texas.

343. Hansberry, Lorraine (1930-1965). *To Be Young, Gifted and Black: Lorraine Hansberry in Her Own Words.* Adapted, Foreword, and Postscript by Robert Nemiroff. Introduction by James Baldwin. Illustrated. Englewood Cliffs, N.J.: Prentice-Hall, 1969. 266p.

Reprinted New York: Signet Books—New American Library, 1970.

DHU   DLC   PLuL   PPi   PPiCl   PPiU   WU

A collection of diary entries, dramatic pieces, short stories, letters, and autobiographical vignettes by the noted playwright reveals her personal life, her childhood in Chicago, and her collegiate years at the University of Wisconsin.

344. Harris, Charles Jacob (1885-   ). *Reminiscences of My Days with Roland Hayes.* Orangeburg, S.C.: The Author, 1944. 27p.

DHU   DLC   NN   OO   PLuL

In this brief pamphlet, the piano accompanist to concert singer Roland Hayes describes their adventures and music performances in Boston, and on tours through New England towns and the South, from 1911 to 1917.

345. Harris, Paul Nelson (1914-   ). *Base Company 16.* New York: Vantage Books, 1963. 201p.

DHU   DLC   NN   WU

In a selection of diary entries dated from October 1943 to December 1945, a former coxswain conveys the story of racism in the U.S. Navy. Personal incidents occurred in California, Hawaii, and the New Hebrides Islands.

346. Harrison, Eddie M. (1942-   ), and Alfred V. J. Prather. *No Time for*

Dying. Introduction by Edward W. Brooke. Interchapters by Alfred
V. J. Prather. Englewood Cliffs, N.J.: Prentice-Hall, 1973. 259p.
  DLC   PPi
  A man who allegedly committed a murder in Washington, D.C., in
1960, speaks of that event, his imprisonment, the trial and retrial of
his case, and the commutation of his sentence by President Richard M.
Nixon in 1970. He also mentions his service as a government antipov-
erty worker after his release from prison.

347. Harrison, Juanita (1891-   ). *My Great, Wide, Beautiful World.*
  Arranged and Preface by Mildred Morris. New York: Macmillan, 1936.
  318p.
    CtH   DHU   MU   OU   OrU   PLuL   PPiU   TxU   ViU   WvU
    A Mississippi woman provides a diary account of her travels as she
  worked her way through twenty-two countries between 1927 and
  1935.

348. Haskins, [James] Jim (1941-   ). *Diary of a Harlem Schoolteacher.*
  Introduction by Rhody McCoy. New York: Grove Press, 1969. 149p.
    Reprinted New York: Evergreen Black Cat Books—Grove Press, 1970.
    CtY   IaU   InU   KU   MiU   NIC   NcU   OkU   PPiU   ViU
    A diary account of the 1967-1968 school year by a Harlem teacher
  of emotionally disturbed and retarded children depicts problems in
  urban education.

349. Holsey, Lucius Henry (1842-1920). *Autobiography, Sermons, Addresses, and Essays.* Introduction by George Williams Walker. Atlanta:
  Franklin Printing & Publishing Co., 1898. 288p.
    DHU   IEG   NN   OClWHi   TNF   WHi
    The brief "Autobiography" section of this collection sketches the
  author's slave life in Georgia; his career as a minister and then a bishop
  in the Colored Methodist Episcopal Church, serving in Georgia, Texas,
  Arkansas, Alabama, and Tennessee; and his efforts to help found Paine
  College (Georgia).

350. Holt, Len W. (1928-   ). *An Act of Conscience.* Appendix. Boston:
  Beacon Press, 1965. 236p.
    CSdS   DHU   FTaFA   FTaSU   NN   PPi   PPiU   WHi   WU   WvU
    A civil rights lawyer analyzes racial attitudes in Danville, Virginia,
  describes the racial protest demonstrations and violence there during the
  summer of 1963, and speaks of his own imprisonment and the ensuing
  court case.

351. Hunton, Addie D. Waites (1875-1943), and Kathryn Magnolis Johnson
  (b. 1878). *Two Colored Women with the American Expeditionary
  Forces.* Illustrated. Notes. Brooklyn: Eagle Press, 1920. 256p.
    Reprinted New York: AMS Press, 1971.
    DHU   MB   MU   MiU   NN   NcD   PLuL   PP   PPiU   WHi
    Two YMCA workers in France during World War I report personal

experiences in their essays on Negro combat units, race relations in
France, and YMCA programs for military personnel.

352. Hurston, Zora Neale (1901-1960). *Tell My Horse*. Illustrated.
Appendix. Philadelphia: Lippincott, 1938. 301p.

    CU   DHU   FTaSU   KU   NN   NcD   OrU   PSt   TU   WU

    This highly personal account of and response to an anthropological
field trip to Jamaica and Haiti in the 1930s stresses local customs,
habits, history, and politics. [See Item 124.]

353. Iceberg Slim—see Beck, Robert.

354. Jackson, George Lester (1941-1971). *Soledad Brother: The Prison
Letters of George Jackson*. Introduction by Jean Genet. New York:
Coward-McCann, 1970. 330p.

    Reprinted New York: Bantam Books, 1970.

    CtHT   DHU   DLC   NN   PPi   PPiCl   PPiU   WvU

    In these letters to relatives, friends, and his lawyer, written from
California prisons between 1964 and 1970, Jackson calls for a national
revolution, while also tracing his intellectual development and growing
political awareness. Briefly described are the author's early life in rural
Illinois, Chicago, and Los Angeles; his criminal activities; and his prison
life. (Jackson was later killed, allegedly attempting to escape from
prison.)

355. Jeter, Henry Norval (1851-1938). *Jeter's Twenty-Five Years' Experience with the Shiloh Baptist Church and Her History*. Preface by
Charles S. Morris. Illustrated. Providence: Remington Printing Co.,
1901. 98p.

    DHU   MB   NN   RPB   WHi

    In this history of a Baptist church in Newport, Rhode Island, from
1875, a minister also mentions his slave life in Virginia and his studies
at Wayland Seminary (Washington, D.C.). [See next item.]

356. Jeter, Henry Norval (1851-1938). *Forty-Two Years Experience as a
Pastor; Evangelical, Humane and Reform Activities. Brief Fifty Years
History of the New England Baptist Convention*. Introduction by
Oliver St. Paul Thompson. Illustrated. N.P. [Providence?]: n.p. [The
Author?], n.d. [1923?]. 48p.

    PCC

    Jeter refers to his Baptist Church activities in Newport, Rhode Island,
offers advice to other ministers, and advocates the church's leadership
in resolving national racial problems. [See preceding item.]

357. Johnson, Kathryn Magnolis—see Hunton, Addie D. Waites.

358. Johnson, William Henry (1833-1901). *Autobiography of Dr. William
Henry Johnson; Respectfully Dedicated to His Adopted Home, the
Capital City of the Empire State*. Preface by James E. Boddy. Illustrated. Appendix. Index. Albany, N.Y.: Argus Co., Printers, 1900.
318p.

Reprinted New York: Haskell House, 1970.

DHU   DLC   NN   NcD   NjP   TxU   WHi

This collection of essays, speeches, and letters on a variety of topics includes references to Johnson's childhood in Virginia and Philadelphia, his activities in the Underground Railroad, his military service during the Civil War, and his life as a journalist, editor, civil rights leader, and worker for the Republican Party in Albany, New York.

359. Jones, Howard Olean (1921-   ). *Shall We Overcome? A Challenge to Negro and White Christians*. Westwood, N.J.: Fleming H. Revell, 1966. 146p.

Reprinted as *For This Time: A Challenge to Negro and White Christians*. Chicago: Moody Press, 1968.

DHU   DLC   NN   PPi   PPiU   WHi   WvU

An evangelical minister examines the role of Christianity in race relations, and refers to his personal experiences in the U.S. and Africa.

360. Jones, LeRoi [later Baraka, Imamu Amiri] (1934-   ). *Home: Social Essays*. New York: William Morrow, 1966. 252p.

CSt   DHU   FTaFA   IU   MiU   NcD   NjP   OrU   PPiCl   PPiU

A collection of essays written between 1960 and 1965 by the playwright, poet, novelist, and political leader traces his political, racial, and psychological development and features a long account of his visit to Cuba in 1960.

361. King, Martin Luther, Jr. (1929-1968). *Stride Toward Freedom: The Montgomery Story*. Illustrated. Appendix. Index. New York: Harper & Row, 1958. 230p.

Reprinted New York: Ballantine Books, 1960.

Reprinted New York: Perennial Library—Harper & Row, 1964.

AU   CtY   DHU   FTaFA   IU   InU   PLuL   PPiCl   PPiU   WaU

The famous civil rights leader and Baptist minister, assassinated in 1968, here portrays the bus boycott he led in Montgomery, Alabama, in 1955 and 1956. He also mentions his youth in Atlanta and his training and education at Morehouse College, the Crozer Theological Seminary (Pennsylvania), and Boston University. [See Item 147.]

362. Lester, Julius (1939-   ). *Search for the New Land: History as Subjective Experience*. New York: Dial Press, 1969. 195p.

Reprinted New York: Laurel Library—Dell, 1970.

DHU   DLC   PPi   PPiCl   PPiU   WU

Lester's "subjective" history of the U.S. after World War II contains letters and journals which also shed light on his youth in Kansas City and Nashville, his college years at Fisk University, and his civil rights work for the Student Nonviolent Coordinating Committee.

363. Little, Malcolm—see Malcolm X.

364. Lucas, Lawrence (1933-   ). *Black Priest/White Church: Catholics and Racism*. New York: Random House, 1970. 270p.

DHU   DLC   PPi   PPiU   WHi   WU   WvU

Often relying on his experiences and observations as a priest in Harlem, Lucas comments on official and unofficial racial attitudes of the Roman Catholic Church.

365. Lynch, John Roy (1847-1939). *The Facts of Reconstruction.* Illustrated. New York: Neale Publishing Co., 1913. 325p.

Reprinted New York: Arno Press, 1968.

Reprinted Indianapolis: Bobbs-Merrill, 1970.

CSdS   CtH   DHU   FTaFA   InU   MB   NN   OTU   PLuL   PPiU

In defending Reconstruction programs, the author mentions his own roles as a citizen and a politician, especially in Mississippi and Washington, D.C. [See Item 158.]

366. Malcolm X [formerly Little, Malcolm] (1925-1965). *Malcolm X Speaks: Selected Speeches and Statements.* Edited, Foreword, and Prefatory Notes by George Breitman. Illustrated. New York: Merit Publishers, 1965. 242p.

Reprinted New York: Grove Press, 1966.

DHU   FTaFA   KU   NN   NcU   NjR   PLuL   PPiCl   PPiU   WaU

These interviews and speeches by the famous racial and religious leader were made during the last year of his life, and they contain many personal references. [See Item 163.]

367. Moore, Gilbert Stuart. *A Special Rage.* Index. New York: Harper & Row, 1971. 276p.

Reprinted New York: Colophon Books—Harper & Row, 1972.

CtH   DLC   PPi   PPiCl   WHi   WU   WvU

A journalist describes the 1968 California murder trial of Black Panther Party leader Huey P. Newton. Moore's report is preceded by a brief account of his youth in Harlem and Jamaica, his education at the College of the City of New York, and his service in the U.S. Army.

368. Morgan, Gordon Daniel (1931-   ). *African Vignettes: Notes of an American Negro Family in East Africa.* Jefferson City, Mo.: New Scholars Press, 1967. 156p.

CSt   CtY   DHU   DLC   GU   ICU   IaU   NNC   PLuL   WU

A professor of sociology at Lincoln University (Missouri) includes personal experiences in his study of East African cultures conducted in 1964 and 1965. [See Item 182.]

369. Morrow, E[verett] Frederic (1909-   ). *Black Man in the White House: A Diary of the Eisenhower Years by the Administrative Officer for Special Projects, the White House, 1955-1961.* Index. New York: Coward-McCann, 1963. 308p.

Reprinted New York: Macfadden Books, 1963.

CSdS   DHU   FTaFA   NN   NcSalL   NjR   PLuL   PPiU   WHi   WvU

Featuring an account of the author's trip to Africa in 1957 with Vice-President Richard M. Nixon, this memoir by a U.S. public official in the White House focuses on his official duties and his relationships with major political, diplomatic, and civil service figures. Personal diary entries are occasionally included. [See Item 183.]

370. Murray, Albert L. (1916-   ). *South to a Very Old Place*. New York: McGraw-Hill, 1971. 230p.

CtH   DLC   PPi   PPiCl   WHi   WU   WvU

Recalling incidents from his early life in Mobile, Alabama, and his college years at Tuskegee Institute, a professor of literature and former major in the U.S. Air Force describes his travels through the South in 1969, often recounting his interviews and conversations with prominent intellectuals and writers, as well as with "ordinary" citizens.

371. Nash, Ide D. (b. 1872). *Bootlegging a Failure and a Lecture to Young Men: My Prison Experience in Oklahoma*. Hugo, Okla.: The Author, 1918. 92p.

DLC

Containing a lecture to young boys on the advantages of a law-abiding life, and advice to young Negroes to pursue careers in agriculture, this pamphlet also portrays the author's bootlegging activities in Oklahoma, other of his criminal involvements, his experiences in prison, and a confession of his reformation.

372. Ottley, Roi (1906-1960). *No Green Pastures*. Bibliography. Index. New York: Scribner's, 1951. 234p.

DHU   DLC   FTaFA   FTaSU   NN   PLuL   PPiCl   PPiU   WU   WvU

Inserting personal anecdotes from his travels in Europe and the Middle East from 1944 to 1946, a journalist and newspaper editor outlines European and Middle Eastern attitudes toward black people, and examines the conditions of blacks in those areas.

373. Owens, [Jones] Jesse [Cleveland] (1913-   ), with Paul Neimark. *I Have Changed*. New York: William Morrow, 1972. 160p.

CtH   DLC   PPi   WvU

The former Olympic track star traces the changes in his racial and political views over a two-year period. He also mentions his early life in Alabama and Cleveland, his track career, and his later life in Chicago and Phoenix. [See Items 189 and 190.]

374. Parks, David (1944-   ). *G I Diary*. Illustrated. New York: Harper & Row, 1968. 133p.

CtY   DHU   MB   MH   MiU   NNC   NcRR   NcU   NjP   PPi

A student at the Rochester Institute of Technology, born the son of Gordon Roger Parks and reared in Minneapolis, here publishes a diary account of his life in the U.S. Army between 1965 and 1967, much of it spent in Vietnam. [See next item and Item 193.]

375. Parks, Gordon Roger (1912-   ). *Born Black*. Illustrated. Philadelphia: Lippincott, 1971. 192p.

CtHT   DHU   DLC   PPi   PPiU   WU   WvU

This collection of personal reflections, eyewitness reports, and interviews with black political leaders and civil rights workers features
numerous photographs by the author. [See preceding item and Item
193.]

376. Parks, Lillian Rogers (1897-   ), with Frances Spatz Leighton. *My
Thirty Years Backstairs at the White House*. Introduction by Frances
Spatz Leighton. New York: Fleet Publishing Corp., 1961. 346p.
    CtY   DHU   GU   InU   KyU   LU   MH   MiU   MsU   NNC
    A maid in the White House from 1919 to 1960 portrays U.S. Presi-
dents and their families, notable national and international public
figures, and her own experiences. [See next item.]

377. Parks, Lillian Rogers (1897-   ), and Frances Spatz Leighton. *It Was
Fun Working at the White House*. Introduction by Frances Spatz
Leighton. Illustrated. New York: Fleet Press Corp., 1969. 208p.
    DLC   PSt
    The author condenses and simplifies, for young readers, her earlier
book, covering her years as a maid in the White House. She adds a
chapter to describe her return to the White House as a dinner guest
of President Lyndon B. Johnson. [See preceding item.]

378. Patterson, Louis H., Jr. *Life and Works of a Negro Detective*. Illustrated. Dayton, Ohio: The Author, n.d. [1918?]. 132p.
    DHU   NN
    Patterson recalls the details of a few important cases in his career as
a private detective in Dayton, Ohio, preceding his account with a short
sketch of his youth in Ohio, his experiences as a professional   bicycle
racer, and his business activities, particularly in Indianapolis and
Dayton.

379. Paynter, John Henry (1862-1947). *Joining the Navy or Abroad with
Uncle Sam*. Illustrated. Hartford, Conn.: American Publishing Co.,
1895. 298p.
    DHU   DLC   NN   PPiU
    A cabin boy in the U.S. Navy describes his global adventures in
1894, also briefly mentioning his boyhood in Delaware and Washington, D.C., and his education at Lincoln University (Pennsylvania).
[See next two items.]

380. Paynter, John Henry (1862-1947). *Fifty Years After*. Illustrated. New
York: Margent Press, 1940. 224p.
    DHU   DLC   FTaFA   NN   PLuL   PP
    Essays on a variety of topics, including literature, are accompanied
by some of the author's poems and an account of his visits to England
and Paris in the 1930s. [See preceding item and next item.]

381. Paynter, John Henry (1862-1947). *Horse and Buggy Days with Uncle
Sam*. Illustrated. New York: Margent Press, 1943. 190p.
    DHU   FTaFA   NN   PLuL   PP   WHi

Examining the problems of Negroes in U.S. Civil Service jobs, the author also depicts his life in Denver as a janitor, newspaper worker, and U.S. Postal Service employee; and his work for thirty-nine years with the Internal Revenue Bureau of the U.S. Department of the Treasury. [See preceding two items.]

382. Ransom, Reverdy Cassius (1861-1959). *School Days at Wilberforce*. Illustrated. Springfield, Ohio: New Era Co., 1892. 66p.

DHU   NN   OWibfU

Occasionally inserting comments about his own student experiences at Wilberforce University, Ransom describes the goals, the academic programs, and the physical plant of the University during the 1880s. [See Item 210.]

383. Redding, J[ay] Saunders (1906-   ). *No Day of Triumph*. Introduction by Richard Wright. New York: Harper & Bros., 1942. 342p.

CSdS   DHU   FTaSU   NN   PLuL   PPi   PPiU   WHi   WU   WvU

The major part of Redding's book conveys his impressions and observations during a journey through the Southern states in 1940. This account is preceded by a brief autobiographical sketch of his youth in Wilmington, Delaware, his education at Brown University, and his teaching career at Morehouse College. [See next two items.]

384. Redding, J[ay] Saunders (1906-   ). *On Being a Negro in America*. Indianapolis: Bobbs-Merrill, 1951. 156p.

CSdS   CtH   DHU   FTaSU   NcSalL   OTU   PLuL   PPiCl   PPiU   WvU

A teacher, scholar, essayist, and fiction writer publishes an extended essay on racial problems, also representing some of the incidents and events of his own life. [See preceding item and next item.]

385. Redding, J[ay] Saunders (1906-   ). *An American in India: A Personal Report on the Indian Dilemma and the Nature of Her Conflicts*. Indianapolis: Bobbs-Merrill, 1954. 277p.

DHU   FTaFA   MB   NN   OCl   OOxM   PLuL   PPiU   TxU   ViU

Redding's account of his lecture tour and travels in India in 1952 contains personal experiences and analyses of Indian sociopolitical issues. [See preceding two items.]

386. Reed, Willis (1942-   ), with Phil Pepe. *A View from the Rim: Willis Reed on Basketball*. Illustrated. Philadelphia: Lippincott, 1971. 208p.

DLC   PPi

A professional basketball player for the New York Knickerbockers writes a handbook on basketball, a report and appreciation of his teammates and some opposing players, and a sketch of his youth in Louisiana, his years at Grambling College, and his athletic career.

387. Robeson, Eslanda Cardoza Goode (1896-1965). *African Journey*. Illustrated. New York: John Day, 1945. 154p.

DHU   DLC   FTaFA   FTaSU   NN   PLuL   PPi   PPiU   WvU

The details and discoveries of an anthropological field trip to Africa in 1936 are recorded here in journal form. [See Item 213.]

388. Rowan, Carl Thomas (1925-   ). *South of Freedom.* New York: Knopf, 1952. 270p.

    CSdS   CtH   DHU   FTaFA   MB   OU   PLuL   PPiU   TU   TxU

    A journalist and U.S. Government official tells of his trip through the South in 1951, referring occasionally to his boyhood in Tennessee.

389. Rustin, Bayard (1910-   ). *Down the Line: The Collected Writings of Bayard Rustin.* Introduction by C. Vann Woodward. Index. Chicago: Quandrangle Books, 1971. 355p.

    CtH   DLC   PPi   PPiU   WHi   WU   WvU

    These diary entries, letters, speeches, and essays by the nationally known civil rights leader were written between 1942 and 1971, but most are from the 1960s.

390. Schuyler, Philippa Duke (1932-1967). *Good Men Die.* Foreword by Daniel Lyons. Bibliography. New York: Twin Circle Publishing Co., 1969. 256p.

    MH   MiU   PPiU   WHi

    Later killed in a helicopter accident in Vietnam, the author here writes of her experiences as a war correspondent there in 1966 and 1967. [See Items 228 and 229.]

391. Shackelford, Otis M. (b. 1871). *Seeking the Best.* Kansas City, Mo.: Franklin Hudson Publishing Co., 1909. 177p.

    Reprinted Kansas City, Mo.: Burton Publishing Co., 1911.

    Reprinted in Shackelford's *Lillian Simmons; or the Conflict of Sections.* Kansas City, Mo.: R. M. Rigby Printing Co., 1918.

    DLC   MH   NN   NcD

    A poet, fiction writer, and teacher publishes some of his poems and essays, and provides a short autobiographical sketch covering his youth in Missouri, his job as a railroad porter, his education at Lincoln Institute (Missouri), and his years as a teacher in Missouri and at Lincoln Institute.

392. Smith, Ed (1937-   ). *Where To, Black Man?* Chicago: Quadrangle Books, 1967. 221p.

    DHU   FTaFA   ICU   NIC   NjP   PLuL   PPiU   WHi   WU   WvU

    A U.S. Peace Corps worker in Ghana publishes a diary account of his experiences there in 1963 and 1964.

393. Smith, William Gardner (1926-   ). *Return to Black America.* Englewood Cliffs, N.J.: Prentice-Hall, 1970. 185p.

    CtY   DHU   GU   ICU   InU   MB   MnU   NcU   PPiU   WaU

    Smith, an expatriate novelist living in France, recounts his experiences, conversations, and impressions of his 1967-1968 travels in many areas of the U.S. He also recalls incidents from his life in Europe and Africa.

394. Sowell, Thomas (1930-   ). *Black Education: Myths and Tragedies.*

Notes. Index. New York: McKay, 1972. 338p.

CtH   DLC   PPi   PPiCl   PPiU

An economist and university professor treats problems in the education of blacks, especially at the college level. The first one-third of his book is an autobiographical piece mentioning his youth in Charlotte, North Carolina, and Harlem; his education at Howard University, Harvard University, Columbia University, and the University of Chicago; and his teaching experiences at Rutgers University, Howard University, Cornell University, Brandeis University, and the University of California at Los Angeles.

395. Stone, [Charles] Chuck [Sumner, Jr.]. *Tell It Like It Is*. New York: Trident Press, 1968. 211p.

Reprinted New York: Pocket Books, 1970.

CSt   CoU   CtY   DHU   IaU   NIC   NjR   OU   OrU   PPi

A journalist and newspaper editor reprints a collection of his articles published between 1959 and 1964. He addresses racial problems and issues, often referring to his private life, his career, his youth in Hartford, Connecticut, and his education at Wesleyan University (Connecticut).

396. Sullivan, Leon H. (1922-   ). *Build Brother Build*. Illustrated. Index. Philadelphia: Macrae Smith, 1969. 192p.

CU   DLC   ICU   MB   MH   NjR   PLuL   PPi   PPiU   WU

A businessman and the founder of the Opportunities Industrialization Centers, which train unskilled workers, tells the story of his organization in Philadelphia, and alludes to his childhood in Charleston, West Virginia, his religious studies at the Union Theological Seminary, and his Baptist Church work in Harlem, Philadelphia, and New Jersey.

397. Taylor, Douglas. *World of a Pullman Porter*. Illustrated. New York: n.p. [The Author?], n.d. [1962?]. 48p.

DHU

A railroad porter publishes a pamphlet on his trips across the U.S. during World War II.

398. Teague, [Robert] Bob [L.] (1929-   ). *Letters to a Black Boy*. New York: Walker, 1968. 211p.

Reprinted New York: Lancer Books, 1969.

CtH   CtY   ICU   NcRR   NjP   NjR   PLuL   PPiU   WU   WvU

A journalist and television commentator in New York City prints letters to his son, usually treating the racial implications of private and public affairs. He refers in these letters to his early life in Milwaukee, his college years at the University of Wisconsin, his military service in the U.S. Navy, and his careers.

399. Thompson, Era Bell. *Africa: Land of My Fathers*. Garden City, N.Y.: Doubleday, 1954. 281p.

DHU   FTaSU   MB   NN   OCl   OU   PLuL   PP   PPiU   TxU

A journalist reports the events and impressions of her visit to eighteen African countries in 1953. [See Item 259.]

400. Thorne, Jack [pseud. for Fulton, David Bryant] (b. 1863). *Recollections of a Sleeping Car Porter*. Jersey City, N.J.: Doan & Pilson, 1892. 45p.

DLC   NcU

Working first out of Jersey City, then Chicago, a railroad sleeping-car porter describes some of his experiences with passengers, comments on the countryside he saw, and discourses about race relations.

401. Turner, Zatella Rowena (1906-   ). *My Wonderful Year*. Preface by Margaret Lynn. Boston: Christopher Publishing House, 1939. 117p.

DHU   DLC   NN

A student from Kansas City, Kansas, recalls her experiences at the University of London in 1935 and 1936 and describes the European tourist attractions she visited.

402. Vance, Samuel (1939-   ). *The Courageous and the Proud*. New York: Norton, 1970. 166p.

DHU   DLC   PPi   WHi   WU

A sergeant in the U.S. Army, born and reared in Georgia, Vance pays special attention to the attitudes and conditions of blacks in the Army, while also recalling his military life in Vietnam in 1965 and 1966.

403. Walker, Margaret (1915-   ). *How I Wrote* Jubilee. Introduction by Gloria Gayles. Chicago: Third World Press, 1972. 36p.

DLC   PPiCl

In a pamphlet, a poet and fiction writer remembers the many years of contemplation, planning, research, and writing that went into the publication of her novel *Jubilee* (1966). In doing so, she mentions her youth in Birmingham, Alabama, and New Orleans; her education at Northwestern University and the University of Iowa; her life in West Virginia and North Carolina; and her teaching years at Jackson State College.

404. Washington, Booker Taliaferro (1856-1915). *Working with the Hands: Being a Sequel to "Up from Slavery," Covering the Author's Experiences in Industrial Training at Tuskegee*. Illustrated. New York: Doubleday, Page, 1904. 246p.

Reprinted New York: Arno Press, 1969.

Reprinted New York: Negro Universities Press, 1969.

DHU   DLC   FTaFA   NN   PLuL   PPi   PPiU   WHi   WvU

In publicizing the history, programs, and philosophy of his school, the famous principal of Tuskegee Institute also alludes to his own activities and contributions. [See next item and Items 269, 270, and 271.]

405. Washington, Booker Taliaferro (1856-1915). *The Booker T. Washington Papers*. Vol. 2, *1860-89*. Edited by Louis R. Harlan et al.

Introduction by Louis R. Harlan. Illustrated. Bibliography. Index. Urbana: Univ. of Illinois Press, 1972. 557p.

DLC   IU   PPiCl   WvU

Included here are many of Washington's essays, articles, and private and public letters, written between 1860 and 1889. In them he often refers to his student days at Hampton Institute and to his administrative duties at Tuskegee Institute. [See preceding item and Items 269, 270, and 271.]

406. Williams, Fenton A. (1940-   ). *Just Before the Dawn: A Doctor's Experiences in Vietnam*. Illustrated. New York: Exposition Press, 1971. 127p.

DLC   PPiCl   WHi

A physician and former U.S. Army doctor comments on racial matters and argues his case against U.S. military involvement in Vietnam, while also outlining his own experiences there in 1968 and 1969.

407. Williams, John Alfred (1925-   ). *This Is My Country Too*. New York: Signet Books—New American Library, 1965. 158p.

CSdS   DHU   FTaFA   MH   MiU   NN   OU   PLuL   PPiU   WHi

Through the sponsorship of a national magazine, this novelist traveled across the U.S. in 1963 and 1964 to sample national and regional racial attitudes. His book is a report of his experiences. [See next item.]

408. Williams, John Alfred (1925-   ). *Flashbacks: A Twenty-Year Diary of Article Writing*. Garden City, N.Y.: Anchor Press—Doubleday, 1973. 440p.

DLC   PPiCl   PPiU

In printing essays and articles written between the early 1950s and 1971, the fiction writer, essayist, and journalist refers to his careers; his youth in Mississippi and Syracuse, New York; his education at Syracuse University; his service in the U.S. Navy; his experiences in New York City; and his travels in Europe, Africa, and Israel. [See preceding item.]

409. Williams, Maria P. *My Work and Public Sentiment*. Illustrated. Kansas City, Mo.: Burton Publishing Co., 1916. 272p.

DHU   NN

In a collection of letters, speeches, and essays on various topics, as well as in third-person autobiographical vignettes, the author alludes to her Texas childhood and teaching experiences, her newspaper work in Kansas City, her activities for the Republican Party, and her participation in civic organizations.

410. Wills, [Maurice] Maury [Morning] (1932-   ). *It Pays To Steal*. As told to Steve Gardner. Introduction by Bobby Bragan. Illustrated. Englewood Cliffs, N.J.: Prentice-Hall, 1963. 186p.

CtH   DHU   DLC   NN   PPi

A professional baseball player mixes observations on the sport and

on some of its players with references to his career with the Los
Angeles Dodgers and his boyhood in Washington, D.C.

411. Wright, Charles Stevenson (1932-   ). *Absolutely Nothing to Get
Alarmed About*. New York: Farrar, Straus & Giroux, 1973. 215p.

   DLC   PPiCl   PPiU

In impressionistic short pieces starting in 1967, a fiction writer
depicts his childhood in Missouri, his U.S. Army service in Korea, his
writing career, and, particularly, his adventures in New York City.

412. Wright, Charlotte Crogman (1897-1959). *Beneath the Southern Cross:
The Story of an American Bishop's Wife in South Africa*. New York:
Exposition Press, 1955. 184p.

   DHU   DLC   NN   NcD   NcRR   WU

The wife of Richard Robert Wright, Jr., recalls her experiences in
South Africa from 1936 to 1940, also commenting on African customs, politics, and religious practices. [See Item 290.]

413. Wright, Richard Nathaniel (1908-1960). *How "Bigger" Was Born: The
Story of Native Son, One of the Most Significant Novels of Our Time,
and How It Came To Be Written*. New York: Harper & Bros., 1940.
39p.

Reprinted in *Black Voices: An Anthology of Afro-American Literature*. Edited by Abraham Chapman. New York: Mentor Books—New
American Library, 1968. Pp. 538-563.

Reprinted in *Richard Wright's* Native Son*: A Critical Handbook*.
Edited by Richard Abcarian. Belmont, Cal.: Wadsworth Publishing Co.,
1970. Pp. 14-35.

Reprinted in *Backgrounds to Blackamerican Literature*. Edited by
Ruth Miller. Scranton, Pa.: Chandler Publishing Co., 1971. Pp. 197-
217.

   DLC   NN

A poet and novelist explains in a pamphlet how he conceived and
wrote his famous novel *Native Son* (1940). He mentions people and
incidents that made an impression on his imagination when he lived
in Mississippi and Chicago. [See next four items and Item 289.]

414. Wright, Richard Nathaniel (1908-1960). *Black Power: A Record of
Reactions in a Land of Pathos*. New York: Harper & Bros., 1954.
358p.

   CtHT   DHU   FTaFA   NN   PLuL   PPi   PPiCl   PPiU   WU   WvU

Wright's tour of the African Gold Coast in 1953 results in this sociopolitical commentary, with reports of his personal experiences there.
[See preceding item, next three items, and Item 289.]

415. Wright, Richard Nathaniel (1908-1960). *The Color Curtain: A Report
of the Bandung Conference*. Foreword by Gunnar Myrdal. Cleveland:
World Publishing Co., 1956. 221p.

   CU   CtY   DHU   IU   MiU   NcD   PPiCl   PPiU   TU   TxU

Reporting and analyzing the conference of African and Asian leaders held in Indonesia in 1955, Wright's text also includes interviews and personal experiences. [See preceding two items, next two items, and Item 289.]

416. Wright, Richard Nathaniel (1908-1960). *Pagan Spain*. New York: Harper & Bros., 1957. 241p.

     CU CtY DHU KU MiU MnU OrU PPiCl PPiU ViU

     In his sociopolitical portrait of Spain, Wright also recounts the adventures of his travels there in 1954 and 1955. [See preceding three items, next item, and Item 289.]

417. Wright, Richard Nathaniel (1908-1960). *Letters to Joe C. Brown*. Edited and Introduction by Thomas Knipp. Kent, Ohio: Kent State Univ. Libraries, 1968. 16p.

     DHU DLC MH MnU NjP PLuL PPiU WU WvU

     This pamphlet collects ten-letters from Wright to a friend, written between 1938 and 1945 from New York City, Mexico, and Canada. [See preceding four items and Item 289.]

III. Recent printings of autobiographies and autobiographical books written before 1865: A checklist

418. Allen, Richard. *The Life, Experience, and Gospel Labors.* 1833. 69p.
    Reprinted Nashville: Abingdon Press, 1960.
419. Asher, Jeremiah. *Incidents in the Life of the Rev. J. Asher, Pastor of Shiloh (Coloured) Baptist Church, Philadelphia, U.S.A. and a Concluding Chapter of Facts Illustrating the Unrighteous Prejudice Existing in the Minds of American Citizens Toward Their Coloured Brethren.* 1850. 80p.
    Reprinted Freeport, N.Y.: Books for Libraries Press, 1971.
420. Ball, Charles. *Slavery in the United States: A Narrative of the Life and Adventures of Charles Ball, a Black Man, Who Lived Forty Years in Maryland, South Carolina and Georgia, as a Slave Under Various Masters, and Was One Year in the Navy with Commodore Barney During the Late War.* 1837. 517p.
    Reprinted Detroit: Negro History Press, 1969.
    Reprinted New York: Kraus Reprint Co., 1969.
    Reprinted New York: Negro Universities Press, 1969.
421. Ball, Charles. *Fifty Years in Chains; or, the Life of an American Slave.* 1858. 430p.
    Reprinted Miami, Fla.: Mnemosyne Publishing Co., 1969.
    Reprinted Gloucester, Mass.: Peter Smith Publisher, 1970.
    Reprinted New York: Dover Publications, 1970.
422. Beckwourth, James P. *The Life and Adventures of James P. Beckwourth.* 1856. 405p.
    Reprinted New York: Arno Press, 1969.
    Reprinted Lincoln, Neb.: Univ. of Nebraska Press, 1972.
423. Bibb, Henry. *Narrative of the Life and Adventures of Henry Bibb, an American Slave.* 1850. 208p.
    Reprinted Miami, Fla.: Mnemosyne Publishing Co., 1969.
    Reprinted New York: Negro Universities Press, 1969.
    Reprinted Philadelphia: Rhistoric Publications, 1969.
    Reprinted in *Puttin' On Ole Massa.* Edited by Gilbert Osofsky. New York: Harper & Row, 1969. Pp. 53-171.
424. Brown, Henry Box. *Narrative of Henry Box Brown, Who Escaped from Slavery Enclosed in a Box 3 Feet Long and 2 Feet Wide.* 1849. 90p.
    Reprinted Philadelphia: Rhistoric Publications, 1969.
425. Brown, John. *Slave Life in Georgia: A Narrative of the Life, Sufferings, and Escape of John Brown, a Fugitive Slave, Now in England.* Edited by L. A. Chamerovzow. 1855. 250p.
    Reprinted Freeport, N.Y.: Books for Libraries Press, 1971.

426. Brown, William Wells. *Narrative of William W. Brown, Fugitive Slave.* 1817. 110p.
    Reprinted in *Five Slave Narratives: A Compendium.* New York: Arno Press, 1968.
    Reprinted in *Four Fugitive Slave Narratives.* Edited by Robin W. Winks. Reading, Mass.: Addison-Wesley, 1968.
    Reprinted in *Puttin' On Ole Massa.* Edited by Gilbert Osofsky. New York: Harper & Row, 1969. Pp. 175-223.
    Reprinted New York: Johnson Reprint Corp., 1970.
    Reprinted Westport, Conn.: Negro Universities Press, 1970.
427. Browne, Martha Griffiths. *Autobiography of a Female Slave.* 1857. 401p.
    Reprinted Detroit: Negro History Press, 1969.
    Reprinted Miami, Fla.: Mnemosyne Publishing Co., 1969.
    Reprinted New York: Negro Universities Press, 1969.
428. Campbell, Robert. *A Pilgrimage to My Motherland: An Account of a Journey Among the Egbas and Yorubas of Central Africa, in 1859-60.* 1861. 145p.
    Reprinted in *Search for a Place: Black Separation and Africa, 1860.* Edited by Howard H. Bell. Ann Arbor, Mich.: Univ. of Michigan Press, 1969. Pp. 174-250.
429. Clarke, Lewis Garrard. *Narratives of the Sufferings of Lewis and Milton Clarke.* 1846. 144p.
    Reprinted New York: Arno Press, 1969.
430. Craft, William. *Running a Thousand Miles for Freedom; or the Escape of William and Ellen Craft from Slavery.* 1860. 111p.
    Reprinted in *Great Slave Narratives.* Edited by Arna Bontemps. Boston: Beacon Press, 1969. Pp. 270-361.
    Reprinted Miami, Fla.: Mnemosyne Publishing Co., 1969.
    Reprinted New York: Arno Press, 1969.
431. Delany, Martin Robinson. *Official Report of the Niger Valley Exploring Party.* 1861. 75p.
    Reprinted in *Search for a Place: Black Separation and Africa, 1860.* Edited by Howard H. Bell. Ann Arbor, Mich.: Univ. of Michigan Press, 1969. Pp. 25-148.
432. Douglass, Frederick. *Narrative of the Life of Frederick Douglass, an American Slave.* 1845. 125p.
    Reprinted Cambridge, Mass.: Harvard Univ. Press, 1960.
    Reprinted New York: Macmillan, 1962.
    Reprinted New York: Doubleday, 1963.
    Reprinted New York: Signet Books—New American Library, 1968.
    [See next item and Item 66.]
433. Douglass, Frederick. *My Bondage and My Freedom.* 1855. 432p.
    Reprinted New York: Arno Press, 1968.

Reprinted New York: Dover Publications, 1969.
Reprinted Chicago: Johnson Publishing Corp., 1970.
[See preceding item and Item 66.]

434. Equiano, Olaudah. *The Interesting Narrative of the Life of Olaudah Equiano, or Gustavus Vassa, the African*. 1789. 294p.
    Abridged and reprinted New York: Frederick A. Praeger, 1967.
    Reprinted in *Great Slave Narratives*. Edited by Arna Bontemps. Boston: Beacon Press, 1969. Pp. 4-192.
    Reprinted as *The Life of Olaudah Equiano, or Gustavus Vassa, the African*. New York: Negro Universities Press, 1969.

435. Forten [Grimké], Charlotte L. *The Journal of Charlotte L. Forten*. 1854-1864.
    Originally published New York: Dryden Press, 1953. Edited by Ray Allen Billington. 248p.
    Reprinted New York: Collier Books, 1961.
    [See Item 341.]

436. Grandy, Moses. *Narrative of the Life of Moses Grandy, Late a Slave in the United States of America*. 1844. 46p.
    Reprinted New York: Arno Press, 1968.

437. Green, William. *Narrative of Events in the Life of William Green (Formerly a Slave), Written by Himself*. 1853. 23p.
    Reprinted Philadelphia: Rhistoric Publications, 1969.

438. Grimes, William. *Life of William Grimes, the Runaway Slave, Brought Down to the Present Time*. 1855. 93p.
    Reprinted in *Five Black Lives: The Autobiographies of Venture Smith, James Mars, William Grimes, the Rev. G. W. Offley, James L. Smith*. Middletown, Conn.: Wesleyan Univ. Press, 1971. Pp. 59-128.

439. Henson, Josiah. *Truth Stranger Than Fiction: Father Henson's Story of His Own Life*. 1858. 212p.
    Reprinted Reading, Mass.: Addison-Wesley, 1969.
    Reprinted as *Father Henson's Story*. Upper Saddle River, N.J.: Literature House—Gregg Press, 1970.
    Reprinted as *Father Henson's Story of His Own Life*. New York: Corinth Books, 1962.
    Reprinted Chicago: Afro-Am Publishing Co., 1970.
    Reprinted Gloucester, Mass.: Peter Smith Publisher, 1970.
    [See Item 107.]

440. Jackson, Andrew. *Narrative and Writings of Andrew Jackson, of Kentucky; Containing an Account of His Birth, and Twenty-Six Years of His Life While a Slave*. 1847. 120p.
    Reprinted Miami, Fla.: Mnemosyne Publishing Co., 1969.

441. Jacobs, Harriet Brent. *Incidents in the Life of a Slave Girl*. Edited by L. Maria Child. 1861. 306p.
    Reprinted Detroit: Negro History Press, 1969.

Reprinted Miami, Fla.: Mnemosyne Publishing Co., 1969.
Reprinted New York: AMS Press, 1972.

442. Jefferson, Isaac. *Memories of a Monticello Slave; as Dictated to Charles Campbell in the 1840's by Isaac, One of Thomas Jefferson's Slaves.*
Originally published Charlottesville, Va.: Univ. of Virginia Press, 1951. Edited by Rayford W. Logan. 45p.
Reprinted in *Jefferson in Monticello*. Edited by James A. Bear. Charlottesville, Va.: Univ. Press of Virginia, 1967. Pp. 3-24.

443. Johnson, William. *William Johnson's Natchez: The Ante-Bellum Diary of a Free Negro.* 1835-1851.
Originally published Baton Rouge, La.: Louisiana State Univ. Press, 1951. Edited by William Ransom Hogan and Edwin Adams Davis. 812p.

444. Lane, Lunsford. *The Narrative of Lunsford Lane, Formerly of Raleigh, N.C.; Embracing an Account of His Early Life, the Redemption by Purchase of Himself and Family from Slavery, and His Banishment from the Place of His Birth for the Crime of Wearing a Colored Skin.* 1842. 54p.
Reprinted in *Five Slave Narratives: A Compendium*. New York: Arno Press, 1968.

445. Loguen, Jermain Wesley. *The Rev. J. W. Loguen, as a Slave and as a Freeman. A Narrative of Real Life.* 1859. 454p.
Reprinted New York: Negro Universities Press, 1968.

446. Mars, James. *Life of James Mars, a Slave, Born and Sold in Connecticut.* 1864. 38p.
Reprinted Miami, Fla.: Mnemosyne Publishing Co., 1969.
Reprinted Philadelphia: Rhistoric Publications, 1969.
Reprinted in *Five Black Lives: The Autobiographies of Venture Smith, James Mars, William Grimes, the Rev. G. W. Offley, James L. Smith.* Middletown, Conn.: Wesleyan Univ. Press, 1971. Pp. 35-58.

447. Nesbit, William. *Four Months in Liberia; or African Colonization Exposed.* 1855. 84p.
Reprinted in *Two Black Views of Liberia*. New York: Arno Press, 1969.

448. Northup, Solomon. *Twelve Years a Slave.* 1853. 336p.
Reprinted Baton Rouge, La.: Louisiana State Univ. Press, 1968.
Reprinted in *Puttin' On Ole Massa*. Edited by Gilbert Osofsky. New York: Harper & Row, 1969. Pp. 227-406.
Reprinted New York: Dover Publications, 1970.
Reprinted St. Clair Shores, Mich.: Scholarly Press, 1972.

449. Offley, G. W. *A Narrative of the Life and Labors of the Rev. G. W. Offley, a Colored Man, and Local Preacher.* 1860.
Reprinted in *Five Black Lives: The Autobiographies of Venture Smith, James Mars, William Grimes, the Rev. G. W. Offley, James L.*

Smith. Middletown, Conn.: Wesleyan Univ. Press, 1971. Pp. 129-137.

450. Pennington, James W. C. *The Fugitive Blacksmith; or Events in the History of James W. C. Pennington, Pastor of a Presbyterian Church, New York, Formerly a Slave in the State of Maryland, United States*. 1849. 87p.

Reprinted in *Five Slave Narratives: A Compendium*. New York: Arno Press, 1968.

Reprinted in *Great Slave Narratives*. Edited by Arna Bontemps. Boston: Beacon Press, 1969. Pp. 196-267.

Reprinted Westport, Conn.: Negro Universities Press, 1971.

451. Randolph, Peter. *Sketches of Slave Life; or, Illustrations of the Peculiar Institution*. 1855. 82p.

Reprinted Philadelphia: Rhistoric Publications, 1969.

[See Item 209.]

452. Roberts, James. *The Narrative of James Roberts, Soldier in the Revolutionary War and at the Battle of New Orleans*. 1858. 32p.

Reprinted Hattiesburg, Miss.: Book Farm, 1945.

453. Roper, Moses. *A Narrative of the Adventures and Escape of Moses Roper, from American Slavery*. 2d ed. 1838. 108p.

Reprinted Philadelphia: Rhistoric Publications, 1969.

Reprinted New York: Negro Universities Press, 1970.

454. Smith, Venture. *A Narrative of the Life and Adventures of Venture, a Native of Africa, but Resident About Sixty Years in the United States of America*. 1798. 41p.

Reprinted in *Five Black Lives: The Autobiographies of Venture Smith, James Mars, William Grimes, the Rev. G. W. Offley, James L. Smith*. Middletown, Conn.: Wesleyan Univ. Press, 1971. Pp. 1-34.

455. Steward, Austin. *Twenty-Two Years a Slave, and Forty Years a Freeman; Embracing a Correspondence of Several Years, While Resident of Wilberforce Colony, London, Canada West*. 1857. 360p.

Reprinted in *Four Fugitive Slave Narratives*. Edited by Robin W. Winks. Reading, Mass.: Addison-Wesley, 1969.

Reprinted New York: Negro Universities Press, 1969.

Reprinted New York: New American Library, 1969.

456. Thompson, John. *The Life of John Thompson, a Fugitive Slave; Containing His History of 25 Years in Bondage, and His Providential Escape*. 1856. 143p.

Reprinted New York: Negro Universities Press, 1968.

457. Turner, Nat. *The Confessions of Nat Turner, the Leader of the Late Insurrection in Southampton, Va. As Made to Thomas Gray*. 1831. 23p.

Reprinted in *Nat Turner's Slave Rebellion*. By Herbert Aptheker. New York: Humanities Press, 1966. Pp. 127-152.

Reprinted Miami, Fla.: Mnemosyne Publishing Co., 1969.

Reprinted in *Afro-American History: Primary Sources*. Edited by
Thomas R. Frazier. New York: Harcourt, Brace & World, 1970. Pp.
64-75.

Reprinted in *Black Identity: A Thematic Reader*. Edited by Francis
E. Kearns. New York: Holt, Rinehart & Winston, 1970. Pp. 213-225.

Reprinted in *Black Writers of America: A Comprehensive Anthology*.
Edited by Richard Barksdale and Keneth Kinnamon. New York: Macmillan, 1972. Pp. 163-173.

Reprinted New York: AMS Press, 1973.

458. Ward, Samuel Ringgold. *Autobiography of a Fugitive Negro: His Anti-
Slavery Labours in the United States, Canada, & England*. 1855. 320p.

Reprinted New York: Arno Press, 1968.

Reprinted Chicago: Johnson Publication Corp., 1970.

459. Williams, Samuel. *Four Years in Liberia. A Sketch of the Life of the
Rev. Samuel Williams. With Remarks on the Missions, Manners and
Customs of the Natives of Western Africa. Together with an Answer
to Nesbit's Book*. 1857. 66p.

Reprinted in *Two Black Views of Liberia*. New York: Arno Press,
1969.

Library symbols

Each entry item in Sections I and II shows up to ten letter symbols for libraries holding the individual volumes. The letter symbols, together with the libraries they represent, appear below:

AAP	Auburn University, Auburn, Alabama
AU	University of Alabama, University, Alabama
ArU	University of Arkansas, Fayetteville, Arkansas
AzU	University of Arizona, Tucson, Arizona
CLU	University of California at Los Angeles, Los Angeles, California
CSdS	San Diego State College, San Diego, California
CSt	Stanford University, Stanford, California
CU	University of California, Berkeley, California
CU-A	University of California, Davis, California
CoDR	Regis College, Denver, Colorado
CoU	University of Colorado, Boulder, Colorado
CtH	Hartford Public Library, Hartford, Connecticut
CtHT	Trinity College, Hartford, Connecticut
CtY	Yale University, New Haven, Connecticut
DHU	Howard University, Washington, D.C.
DLC	Library of Congress, Washington, D.C.
DNAL	U.S. National Agricultural Library, Washington, D.C.
DNLM	National Library of Medicine, Washington, D.C.
FMU	University of Miami, Coral Gables, Florida
FTaFA	Florida Agricultural and Mechanical University, Tallahassee, Florida
FTaSU	Florida State University, Tallahassee, Florida
GAU	Atlanta University, Atlanta, Georgia
GEU	Emory University, Atlanta, Georgia
GM	Middle Georgia Regional Library, Macon, Georgia
GU	University of Georgia, Athens, Georgia
ICU	University of Chicago, Chicago, Illinois
IEG	Garrett Theological Seminary, Evanston, Illinois
IEdS	Southern Illinois University, Edwardsville, Illinois
IU	University of Illinois, Urbana, Illinois
IaHi	State Historical Society of Iowa, Iowa City, Iowa
IaU	University of Iowa, Iowa City, Iowa
InU	Indiana University, Bloomington, Indiana
KMK	Kansas State University, Manhattan, Kansas
KU	University of Kansas, Lawrence, Kansas
KyBgW	Western Kentucky State College, Bowling Green, Kentucky
KyU	University of Kentucky, Lexington, Kentucky

LN	New Orleans Public Library, New Orleans, Louisiana
LNHT	Tulane University, New Orleans, Louisiana
LU	Louisiana State University, Baton Rouge, Louisiana
MB	Boston Public Library, Boston, Massachusetts
MH	Harvard University, Cambridge, Massachusetts
MU	University of Massachusetts, Amherst, Massachusetts
MdBE	Enoch Pratt Free Library, Baltimore, Maryland
MeB	Bowdoin College, Brunswick, Maine
MiD	Detroit Public Library, Detroit, Michigan
MiEM	Michigan State University, East Lansing, Michigan
MiU	University of Michigan, Ann Arbor, Michigan
MnU	University of Minnesota, Minneapolis, Minnesota
MoSW	Washington University, St. Louis, Missouri
MoU	University of Missouri, Columbia, Missouri
MsU	University of Mississippi, University, Mississippi
N	New York State Library, Albany, New York
NB	Brooklyn Public Library, Brooklyn, New York
NIC	Cornell University, Ithaca, New York
NN	New York Public Library, New York, New York
NNC	Columbia University, New York, New York
NR	Rochester Public Library, Rochester, New York
NRU	University of Rochester, Rochester, New York
NSyU	Syracuse University, Syracuse, New York
Nc	North Carolina State Library, Raleigh, North Carolina
NcD	Duke University, Durham, North Carolina
NcGA	North Carolina Agricultural and Technical State University, Greensboro, North Carolina
NcRR	Richard B. Harrison Public Library, Raleigh, North Carolina
NcSalL	Livingstone College, Salisbury, North Carolina
NcU	University of North Carolina, Chapel Hill, North Carolina
NcWsW	Wake Forest University, Winston-Salem, North Carolina
NjP	Princeton University, Princeton, New Jersey
NjR	Rutgers—The State University, New Brunswick, New Jersey
OC	Public Library of Cincinnati and Hamilton County, Cincinnati, Ohio
OCLloyd	Lloyd Library and Museum, Cincinnati, Ohio
OCl	Cleveland Public Library, Cleveland, Ohio
OClJC	John Carroll University, Cleveland, Ohio
OClWHi	Western Reserve Historical Society, Cleveland, Ohio
OEac	East Cleveland Public Library, East Cleveland, Ohio
OO	Oberlin College, Oberlin, Ohio
OOxM	Miami University, Oxford, Ohio
OTU	University of Toledo, Toledo, Ohio
OU	Ohio State University, Columbus, Ohio

OWibfC   Hallie Q. Brown Library, Central State University, Wilberforce, Ohio
OWibfU   Carnegie Library, Wilberforce University, Wilberforce, Ohio
OkU   University of Oklahoma, Norman, Oklahoma
OrU   University of Oregon, Eugene, Oregon
PCC   Crozer Theological Seminary, Chester, Pennsylvania
PLuL   Lincoln University, Lincoln University, Pennsylvania
PP   Free Library of Philadelphia, Philadelphia, Pennsylvania
PPL   Library Company of Philadelphia, Philadelphia, Pennsylvania
PPPD   Philadelphia Divinity School, Philadelphia, Pennsylvania
PPPrHi   Presbyterian Historical Society, Philadelphia, Pennsylvania
PPT   Temple University, Philadelphia, Pennsylvania
PPi   Carnegie Library, Pittsburgh, Pennsylvania
PPiCl   Carnegie-Mellon University, Pittsburgh, Pennsylvania
PPiU   University of Pittsburgh, Pittsburgh, Pennsylvania
PSt   Pennsylvania State University, University Park, Pennsylvania
PU   University of Pennsylvania, Philadelphia, Pennsylvania
RP   Providence Public Library, Providence, Rhode Island
RPB   Brown University, Providence, Rhode Island
TNF   Fisk University, Nashville, Tennessee
TU   University of Tennessee, Knoxville, Tennessee
TxDaM   Southern Methodist University, Dallas, Texas
TxH   Houston Public Library, Houston, Texas
TxU   University of Texas, Austin, Texas
ViHaI   Hampton Institute, Hampton, Virginia
ViU   University of Virginia, Charlottesville, Virginia
ViW   College of William and Mary, Williamsburg, Virginia
WE   Eau Claire Public Library, Eau Claire, Wisconsin
WHi   State Historical Society of Wisconsin, Madison, Wisconsin
WU   University of Wisconsin, Madison, Wisconsin
Wa   Washington State Library, Olympia, Washington
WaSpG   Gonzaga University, Spokane, Washington
WaU   University of Washington, Seattle, Washington
WvU   West Virginia University, Morgantown, West Virginia

Index of experiences, occupations, and professions

The numbers following each category are entry-item numbers for Sections I and II.

Index of geographical locations and educational institutions

The numbers following each location or institution are entry-item numbers for Sections I and II.

Index of titles